HABITUDES®

IMAGES
THAT FORM
LEADERSHIP
HABITS &
ATTITUDES

BY

DR TIM ELMORE

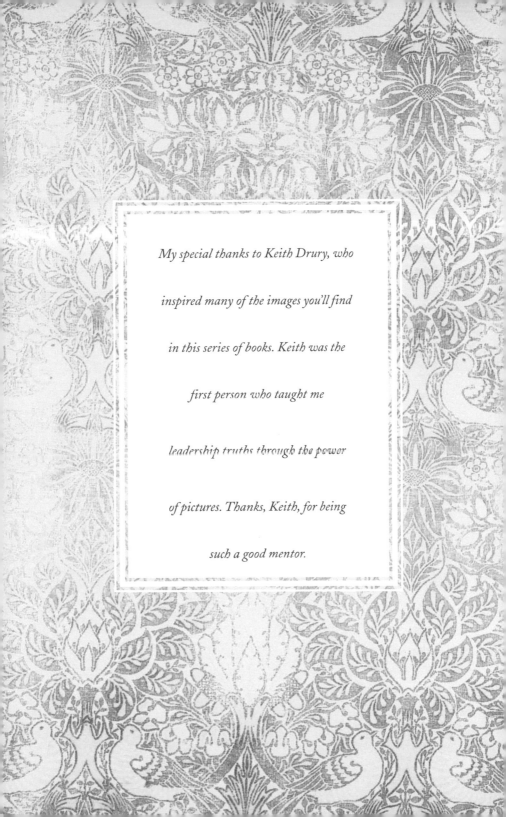

My special thanks to Keith Drury, who

inspired many of the images you'll find

in this series of books. Keith was the

first person who taught me

leadership truths through the power

of pictures. Thanks, Keith, for being

such a good mentor.

All scripture quotations are taken from the New International Version of the Bible. Copyright 1984, 1978, 1973 by International Bible Society. Used by permission of Zondervan Publishing House. All rights reserved.

Published in Atlanta, Georgia by "Growing Leaders, Inc." (www.GrowingLeaders.com)

ISBN: 1-931132-05-4
Printed in the United States of America
Library of Congress Cataloguing-in-Publication Data

TABLE OF CONTENTS

A WORD ABOUT IMAGES

We live in a culture rich with images. We grew up with photographs, TV, movies, video, MTV and DVDs. We can't escape the power of the visual image—and most of us don't want to.

I've learned over my career that most of us are visual learners. We like to see a picture, not just hear a word. Author Leonard Sweet says that images, not words, are the language of the 21st century. Some of the best communicators in history taught using the power of the metaphor and image—from Jesus Christ and His parables to Martin Luther King Jr. and his "I Have a Dream" speech during the Civil Rights movement.

Why? Because pictures stick. We remember pictures long after words have left us. When we hear a speech, we often remember the stories from that speech more than the phrases used by the speaker, because they painted a picture inside of us. They communicate far more than mere words. In fact, words are helpful only as they conjure up a picture in our minds. Most of us think in pictures. If I say the word "elephant" to you, you don't picture the letters e-l-e-p-h-a-n-t, you picture a big gray animal. Pictures are what we file away in our minds. They enable us to store huge volumes of information. There's an old phrase that has stood the test of time: A picture is worth a thousand words. I believe it's true. I pursued a degree in both commercial art as well as theology in college. That's when I recognized the power of the image. Now I get to combine the power of teaching leadership truths with the power of pictures. I hope they linger in your mind and heart. I hope you discover layers of reality in them as you grow. I trust they'll impact you as profoundly as they have me.

This book is part of a series, designed to furnish pictures you can discuss with a community of people. Each picture contains layers of reality, and your discussion can go as deep as you allow it to go. The books are created to guide you on your leadership journey. They are based on the fact that leadership isn't merely one-dimensional. It runs 360 degrees. We influence others all around us. We must first lead ourselves. Then, we will influence those above us. Next, we will influence those around us. Finally, we influence those for whom we are responsible. This book covers self-leadership, because the leadership journey should always begin here. Once I lead myself well, others will be magnetically attracted to follow. Influence naturally ripples from strong character. I won't have to force others to follow me.

Some sociologists describe this generation as EPIC: Experiential, Participatory, Image-driven and Connected. If that's true, I believe we'll get the most out of resources that give us an image, an experience, and a way to connect with each other. Each of these books provides you with not only an image, but also a handful of discussion questions, a self-assessment and an exercise in which you can participate. Dive in and experience each one of them. My hope is that they become signposts that guide you, warn you, and inform you. May they illuminate your leadership journey.

Dr. Tim Elmore

IMAGE ONE
[THE ICEBERG]

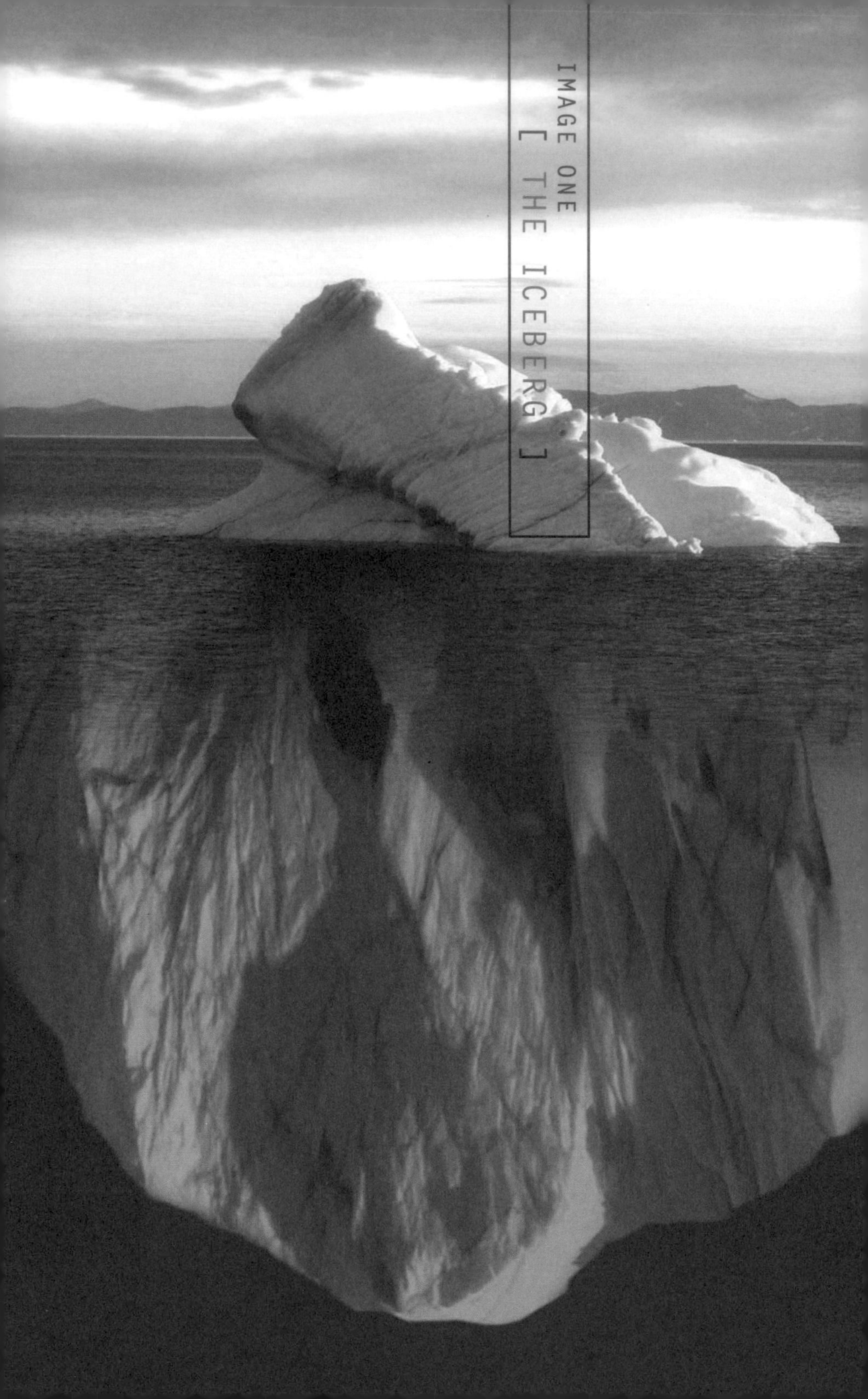

The Iceberg

THE ICEBERG REPRESENTS YOUR LEADERSHIP. THE 10% ABOVE THE WATER IS YOUR SKILL. THE 90% BELOW THE WATER IS YOUR CHARACTER. IT'S WHAT'S BELOW THE SURFACE THAT SINKS THE SHIP.

An iceberg is an interesting picture of the first rule of leadership. There's more to it than meets the eye. Most of an iceberg is below the surface of the water. You probably remember the awesome story of the *Titanic.* (Maybe you saw the movie!) The huge and unsinkable ship received five iceberg warnings that fateful night of April 14, 1912, just before it went down. When the sixth message came in during the wee hours of the next morning: "Look out for icebergs," the operator wired back, "Shut up! I'm busy." These were his last words over the wire before it all happened. Exactly thirty minutes later, the great vessel—the one whose captain said even God couldn't sink— was sinking. Hundreds of passengers and crew were drowned.

What was the problem? They forgot the truth about icebergs. What they saw above the water couldn't have sunk the great ship. Unfortunately they forgot that most of an iceberg is below the water line. They underestimated the power of the iceberg, and overestimated their own strength. What an accurate description of so many leaders today.

The iceberg is a great picture of leadership because so much of our influence comes from qualities we can't see on the outside. It's stuff below the surface. I estimate 90% of our leadership is made up from our character. And, our character is the sum total of our:

• Self-discipline (The ability to do what's right even if you don't feel like it)

• Core values (Principles you live by that enable you to take a moral stand)

• Sense of identity (A realistic self-image based on who God made you to be)

• Emotional security (The capacity to be emotionally stable and consistent)

ple make it into the limelight, and neglect their character. Your skill
ou to the top—but it's your character that will keep you there. If you
strong character, you will eventually sabotage your leadership. You can
only fake it so long. We learned this in the 1980s when so many Christian
televangelists fell morally. We learned it again in the 1990s when many politicians
fell morally, including our president. We learned it again during the first decade
of the new century when corporations such as Enron, WorldCom and Tyco
committed moral crimes and pro athletes were taken to court due to lack of
character. You'd think we would have learned our lesson…but we didn't. As we
entered the second decade of the 21st century, we heard stories of Tiger Woods
cheating on his wife multiple times and Lance Armstrong cheating on his sport
by taking performance-enhancing drugs. What's worse is, many of these people
then lied about it all. My explanation? The iceberg. Weak character may begin
when we are young, with lying and cheating on tests. It eventually takes the form
of fraud, sex crimes, robbery and scandals. The Wall Street meltdown that came
to light in 2008 is still affecting business in America today. The financial crisis
we experienced was not due to a skill problem. It's a character problem. The
scandals all happened in spite of the new legislation to combat corporate crimes.
In other words, we didn't learn our lesson from Enron, back in 2002. We've had
no moral compass.

It didn't start with our generation, though. About a hundred years ago, a boy grew
up in Europe. His father's given name was Alois Schicklgruber. As a teen, he never
learned about character. His parents never taught him right from wrong, so he
began to come up with his own ideas and values. His father put him down when
he talked about becoming a priest, and laughed at him when he spoke of being
an artist. He was never valued, nor taught values. One night, he heard his mom
and dad argue about moving away. Believing they hated him, he suspected they'd
leave him behind. In anger, he put up an emotional wall and never let anyone get
close. He later ran away. This boy grew up to be a man. The man became a leader.
You know him as Adolf Hitler.

History proves that Adolf Hitler was a great leader, but he wasn't a good one. He
failed to use his influence well. His skill and charisma were huge. His character was
horribly flawed. He sabotaged himself—but not until he had slaughtered more than
six million innocent people along the way. Leadership skills are important, but God
doesn't want your skills at the expense of your character and integrity. Lead yourself
well before you try leading others. It is interesting to me that Americans spend an
average of 10% of their life preparing for the 90% that makes up their career. Jesus
Christ, in contrast, spent 90% preparing His inward life, for the 10% that made up
His career. We are in such a hurry today that we blitz through our prep work to
get to the productivity. Sadly, we often cannot sustain a life of character, and fail
morally along the way.

Those who live among icebergs remind us there is such a thing as an iceberg with
very little below the surface, like a floating ice cube. Most of its mass is up top, as

though it is upside down. It's called a "whistler." You can always tell "whistlers" from other icebergs. They constantly drift, and they make a lot of noise. Sound familiar?

The bad news about icebergs is that it's what's below the surface that sinks a ship. When we have weak character, it will eventually damage our ability to lead. The good news is that it's what's below the surface that supports the tip. In the same way, strong character will hold you up long enough to use your skills.

A Look at the Book

Check out Luke 6:43-45 in your Bible. It says:

> 43) For there is no good tree which produces bad fruit; nor, on the other hand, a bad tree which produces good fruit. 44) For each tree is known by its fruit. For men do not gather figs from thorns, nor do they pick grapes from a briar bush. 45) The good man out of the good treasure of his heart brings forth what is good; and the evil man out of the evil treasure brings forth what is evil; for the mouth speaks from that which fills the heart.

These words, spoken by Jesus, are loaded with meaning. We can be sure of at least one conclusion: Whatever happens on the outside of our life stems from what's happening on the inside. When we see the fruit, we know what kind of tree it is; the outside is only a reflection of what's on the inside.

God puts "being" before "doing." He prioritizes taking care of the inside (our heart), because that will determine what takes place on the outside (our behavior).

Why is focusing on the "inside" so difficult for us today?

_____

_____

_____

Why do we put so much emphasis on the "outside" of our lives?

_____

_____

_____

Look at verse 45. The word "treasure" literally means "deposit." What does the word "deposit" mean to you? Try to put this verse into your own words.

_____

_____

_____

Getting Personal

Take a minute and think about your own character. Do you have strong character? On a scale of one to ten (ten being the strongest), rate yourself in the following areas:

1. Self-Discipline (The ability to do what is right even if you don't feel like it)

1   2   3   4   5   6   7   8   9   10

2. Core Values (Principles you live by that enable you to take a moral stand)

1   2   3   4   5   6   7   8   9   10

3. Sense of Identity (A realistic self-image based on who God made you to be)

1   2   3   4   5   6   7   8   9   10

4. Emotional Security (The capacity to be emotionally stable and consistent)

1   2   3   4   5   6   7   8   9   10

Why did you give yourself the scores you did?

_____

_____

_____

_____

Practicing the Truth

Identify several things you really don't like doing. There may be a function around the house, in school or at work. It could be a chore like sweeping the garage or some small task you've procrastinated doing on the job. It may be listening to or interacting with someone who seems unlovable. It might be physical exercise or the discipline of waiting. It could be as simple as eating a vegetable you don't like.

Choose two of these "undesirables" and make them disciplines. Deliberately do what you don't like doing.

Practice them daily for one week. Put them on the calendar and ask someone to hold you accountable to do them. (If you do them daily for two weeks, chances are they will become a habit!)

Afterwards, discuss the results. Did you feel a sense of accomplishment? Did you waver in your commitment? Discuss with someone how daily disciplines pave the way for conquering laziness and indifference. How have you gained personal victory by practicing these disciplines? How does this strengthen your character?

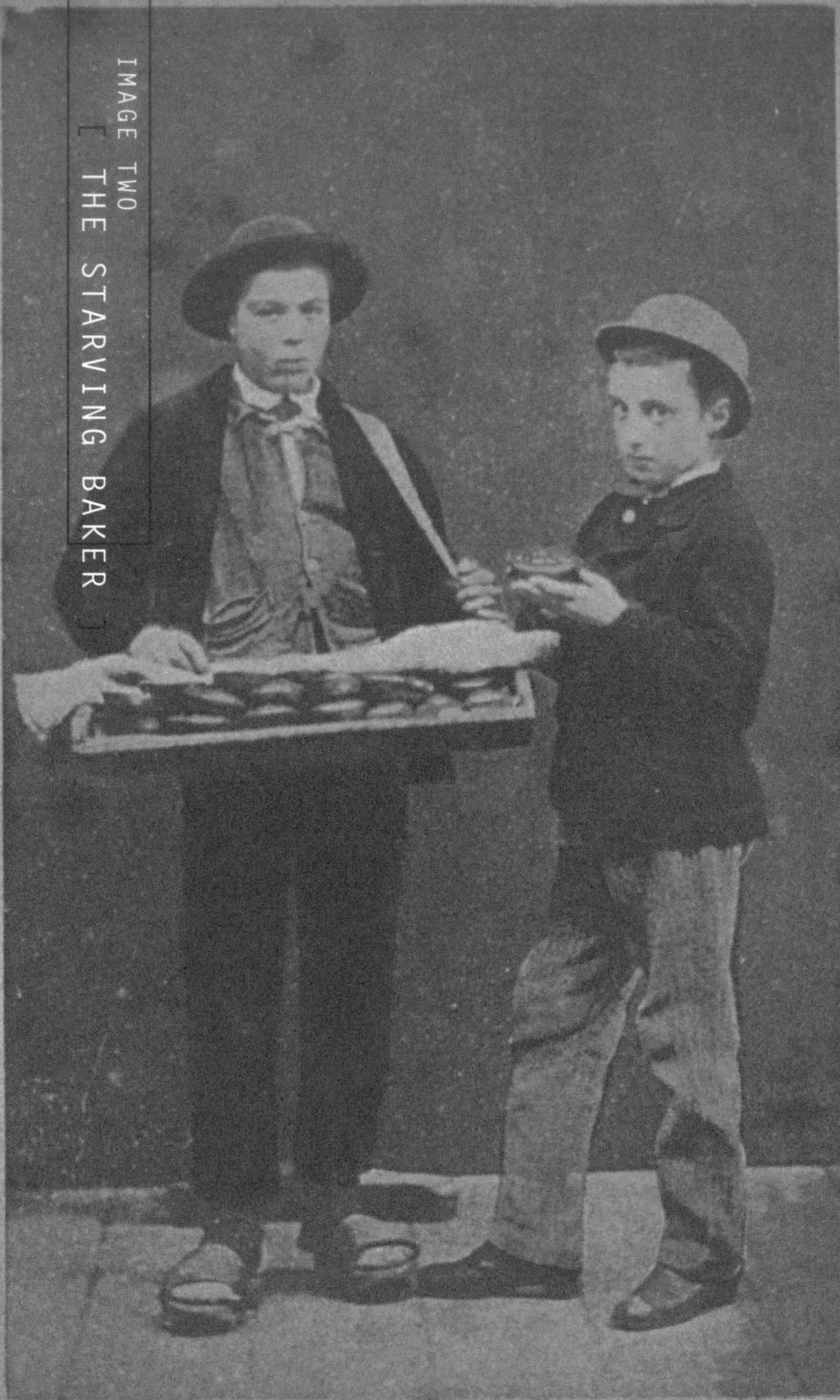

IMAGE TWO

[THE STARVING BAKER]

The Starving Baker

THIS IS A COMMON HAZARD FOR LEADERS. WE'RE LIKE THE BAKER WHO SPENDS SO MUCH TIME BAKING BREAD FOR OTHERS, WE FORGET TO EAT OURSELVES. LEADERS MUST FEED THEMSELVES FOR PERSONAL GROWTH.

Imagine, if you will: you visit a new bagel shop not far from your home. You love going there because the chief baker has created a new recipe for breads, bagels, pastries and cinnamon rolls that are incredible.

Soon, word gets out about this bagel shop. Crowds start forming lines each day, waiting for the new confections to come from this baker's marvelous kitchen. The baker doesn't have enough help, and ends up trying to serve all the customers himself. He is scurrying back and forth, busy with all the requests of the people—but oblivious to what's happening to him. His exhaustion is quickly becoming burnout. What's worse, as you watch him for a few weeks, you see a change. This man is getting thin. Very thin. It almost seems like he is shriveling up. What's up with that?

After observing this baker for a few hours, the problem becomes obvious. This man never stops to eat. The irony is, he is busy serving bread to everyone else, but never stops long enough to feed himself. With food all around him, he is starving. Hmmm. Does this scenario sound familiar?

So many leaders fail to tend to themselves, and eventually are unable to really serve others. They are starving intellectually, emotionally, and spiritually. They can fake it for a while, but eventually they run out of gas. When they do read their Bibles or listen to podcasts, it is always for someone else. They consume information for the "program," but there's no personal growth. They are always preparing some Bible study for a group or a message for others. They neglect to digest the content and apply it to their own lives. Their "talk" is great. Their "walk" becomes fake. They go through the motions but aren't really spending time eating the "bread of life" (John 6:35). They are spiritually starving...so close to food, yet never eating.

The Iceberg reminds us that leaders must lead themselves before leading others. The Starving Baker reminds us that leaders must feed themselves before feeding others.

I wish Jason had learned this principle as a student. During his junior year his attitude went sour. It shocked his friends. He lost any drive to stay involved in his campus ministry, his fraternity and student government. He became bitter, and sometimes took it out on his girlfriend, Lauren. When she finally confronted him about his attitude, he grew quiet at first. Eventually, he confessed he felt like a fake and was tired of trying to be a perfect Christian. The more they talked, the more Lauren could see the reality. Jason wasn't a fake. He just wasn't taking time to invest in his own relationship with Jesus. He burned out because he was depleted, spiritually speaking. His tank was on empty. He had nothing to give. He'd become a "starving baker."

Jason is an interesting contrast to Stacy. Stacy and Jason were students on the same campus. Stacy was busy with both soccer and student government activities, and on top of that led a mentoring group for freshmen girls. Interestingly, Stacy never ran out of gas. Her busy-ness never led to a bad attitude or a critical spirit. Her friends marveled at how she seemed genuinely happy, and although her life was busy, her mind was at peace. How did she accomplish this? It's simple. She took time to feed herself.

She consistently spoke of the former mentor who taught her about "sharpening the axe." This term came from a little story about two lumberjacks who challenged each other to see who could cut down more trees in one day. At daybreak, the first one began furiously chopping down trees. He worked up a sweat early on, and by noon had cut down sixteen trees. The other lumberjack had only cut down four, because he took the first two hours to sharpen his axe. As he sharpened it, his challenger laughed at him knowing he was doomed to lose the bet with all that wasted time.

That's when things got interesting. By early afternoon, the first lumberjack was slowing down. It took him almost an hour to cut one tree down, while his friend was picking up speed. How could this be? Certainly he was as strong as his friend. Unfortunately, strength had little to do with it. It was all about whose axe was sharper. The sharper the axe, the quicker the trees came down. By late afternoon, the second lumberjack who had sharpened his axe had passed his friend by several trees and won easily. Hmmm. It seemed like such a waste of time to sharpen the axe in the morning, but in the long run, it had saved him time and had brought better results. That little story saved Stacy's sanity as a student leader. She took care of herself so she could take care of others.

Lasting leaders practice this truth. President Teddy Roosevelt grew up as a frail kid, and knew his only chance of making a difference was to become a life-long learner. He died in his sleep—and under his pillow was a book he'd been reading right up to his dying day. President Harry Truman grew up as a bit of a nerd, and came to the same conclusion. He built a plan for personal growth and practiced daily reading habits. He later said, "Not all readers are leaders, but all leaders are readers."

The lesson of the Starving Baker? As selfish as it may sound, the most selfless way leaders can serve and grow their people is to tend to their own growth first.

A Look at the Book

Check out Ecclesiastes 10:10 in your Bible. It says:

> *If the axe is dull and he does not sharpen its edge, then he must exert more strength. Wisdom has the advantage of giving success.*

The lumberjack story was inspired by the Scripture above. We all understand the importance of "sharpening the axe." Why do you think we fail to do it? Why does it seem like a waste of time?

_____

_____

_____

Look at the verse above. What is King Solomon saying with this verse? Put it in your own words.

_____

_____

_____

Look up Song of Solomon 1:6. The last sentence of that verse says: *They made me caretaker of the vineyards, but I have not taken care of my own vineyard.* What is the "lesson" of this verse?

_____

_____

_____

Staying "sharp" can mean lots of things. How do you do it? How do you feed and refresh yourself?

_____

_____

_____

Getting Personal

Give yourself a score based on how well you practice the following spiritual disciplines:

1. Devotions (reading the Bible just to connect with God relationally)

1 2 3 4 5 6 7 8 9 10

2. Prayer (talking with God and getting to know Him better through conversation)

1 2 3 4 5 6 7 8 9 10

3. Simplicity (simplifying your life by clearing out the mental and physical clutter)

1 2 3 4 5 6 7 8 9 10

4. Study and meditation (deeper study of the Bible, focusing on certain words or thoughts)

1 2 3 4 5 6 7 8 9 10

5. Worship (taking time to honor God; to tell Him all He's worth; to thank Him; to enjoy His presence)

1 2 3 4 5 6 7 8 9 10

6. Fasting (going without food or some pleasure in order to focus on God and your spiritual growth)

1 2 3 4 5 6 7 8 9 10

Note where you are strong and where you are weak.

PRACTICING THE TRUTH

Try this out for one week. Read a short Scripture from the Bible, and journal three short paragraphs based on what you read. It doesn't have to be long—just jot down your thoughts on these issues:

THEIR TIME: Jot a few sentences on what was being said or done by the original audience. You can almost paraphrase the verses. In your words explain what was happening during their time.

ALL TIME: Now jot a sentence or two on what you think is the all-time principle you can learn from the passage. Is there a timeless truth you can pull from the verses?

MY TIME: Finally, jot down your personal application. What should you do as a result of reading this Scripture? You may want to write out a prayer for yourself.

I suggest you start this discipline by reading one of the Gospels: Matthew, Mark, Luke or John. Take a story from Jesus' life and journal the three paragraphs above. It doesn't have to be a whole chapter, just a story. You might be amazed at what you learn from your journaling.

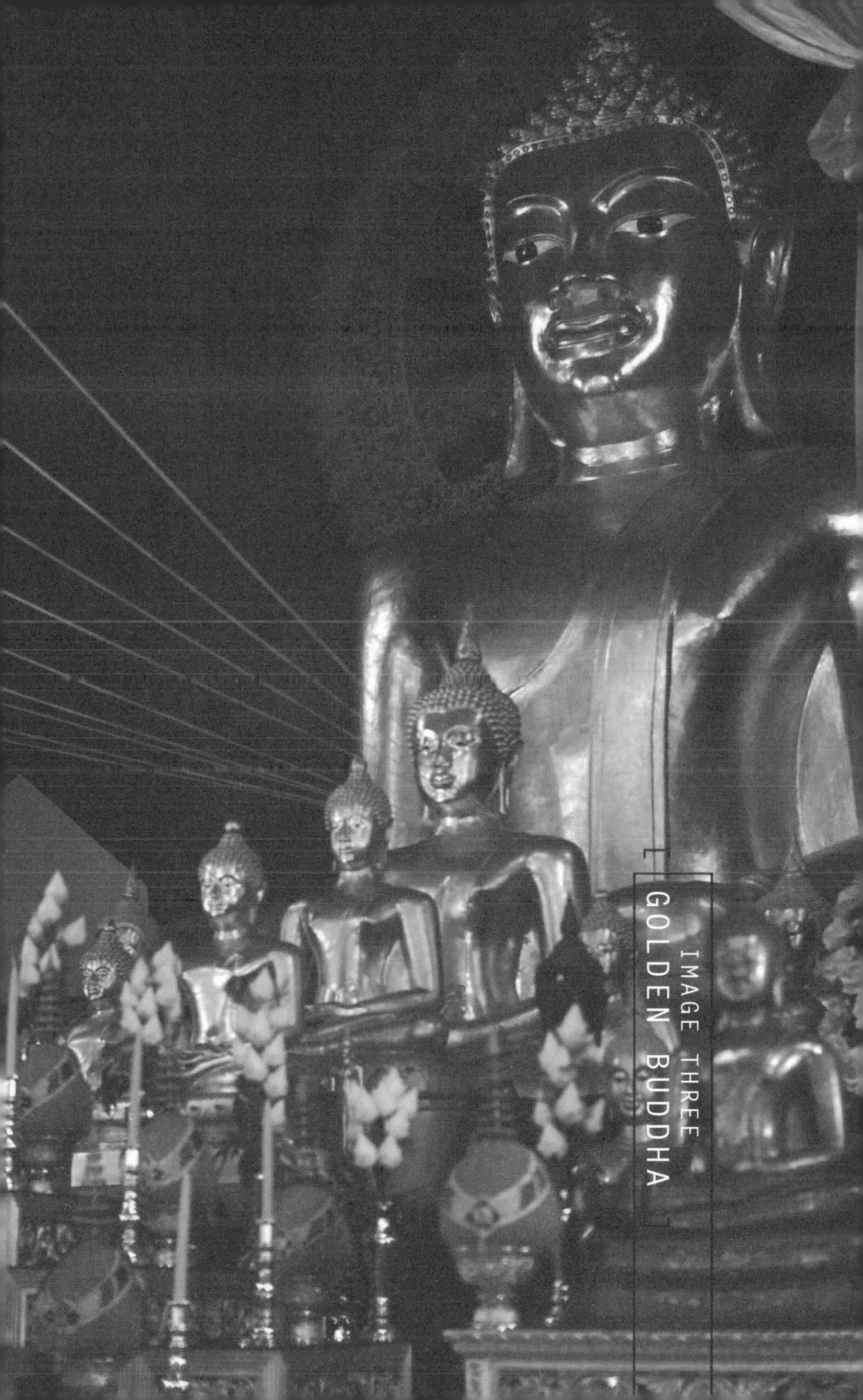

IMAGE THREE
GOLDEN BUDDHA

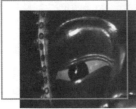

Golden Buddha

LEADERS CANNOT PERFORM WELL IF THEY FAIL TO SEE THE GOLD INSIDE OF THEM. GOOD LEADERS TAKE PERSONAL INVENTORY OF THEIR GOD-GIVEN GIFTS. THIS SHAPES THEIR SELF-IMAGE AND, CONSEQUENTLY, THEIR RESULTS.

Just over fifty years ago, the Golden Buddha was discovered in the city of Bangkok, Thailand. It was an accident. For years, a huge, ugly concrete Buddha sat in the middle of town. Visitors put empty cola cans and other trash at the base of the stained statue; candy wrappers and other waste lay around it. Then one day, a priest decided to move the old statue inside to clean it. In the moving process—it cracked. As the pieces began to crumble, his crew noticed something underneath the concrete shell. They pulled the shell away and were shocked. Inside they found the world's largest chunk of sculptured gold, standing eight feet high!

Wow. For years that huge chunk of gold was there—but no one knew it. Instead, little attention was paid to the statue. It got dirty. Weathered. It was used to store trash. Would this have been done had people recognized what it was storing inside? Everyone was ignorant of the valuable "inventory" the concrete shell contained.

You are a lot like this concrete statue. Your real value is inside, if you would only take inventory of it. Anyone who's worked in a retail store knows what the word "inventory" means. When taking inventory, it means they begin to list the products that are on the shelves. One by one, they count each item until they have an accurate record of what they possess and what they need. Most stores "take inventory" once or twice a year. Some do it every month! In fact, you can't really run a good business without knowing what you've got in your inventory.

When I was in school, I had a friend named Rob, whose first job was to work as a stock clerk in a store. His initial task was to take inventory of what was in the store. I remember Rob got angry at being given such a small job as counting the products. Little did he know—that task would take him three months. It was huge. Taking inventory is no small undertaking, and it pays great dividends. Once you know what you've got, you can go about your business with confidence. The same is true for leaders.

Case in point: There was a young basketball player who got cut from the varsity team during his tenth grade year. It would have been easy for him to evaluate himself as a teen and say, "That's it. I quit." But he didn't. He took a hard look at his strengths and began to develop them. Many believe he became the best player ever. Michael Jordan had to do what all of us have to do. He took inventory. He had to see his skills and talents as the gold on the inside, despite what his coach thought. The same is true for so many influential people in history:

- As a youngster, Walt Disney got fired by a newspaper because he had no good ideas.

- Both Steve Jobs and Bill Gates dropped out of school, feeling like misfits.

- Albert Einstein couldn't speak until he was four years old. He didn't read till he was seven.

- According to Beethoven's music teacher: "As a composer, he is hopeless."

- As a boy, his teachers said Thomas Edison was so stupid he'd never learn anything.

- A coach said Vince Lombardi "…has minimal football knowledge. Lacks motivation."

- Sir Isaac Newton finished next to the lowest in his class and failed geometry.

- After Fred Astaire's first screen test, the MGM director said, "Can't act. Slightly bald. Can dance a little." (Astaire hung that memo in his Beverly Hills home.)

Victor came to the United States from Russia when he was five years old. His parents immediately thrust him into kindergarten. He didn't know the language or the culture he was going to face each day. It was all new and scary. Because he was intimidated, Victor appeared slow to his teachers. He was criticized by classmates.

By his sophomore year in high school, he was emotionally devastated by the judgments he received. Victor concluded that he should give up on school, and try to get a job. So, at sixteen years old, he dropped out of school and began to work odd jobs, just to make ends meet. All he did was survive for about fourteen years. Then, at thirty years old, something interesting happened. Victor took an aptitude test and discovered his IQ was 161. He was shocked. He was a genius. That day changed his life. His true story was written up several times. In fact, Victor Serebriakoff began a great career, obtaining patents for inventions, before starting a family of his own. He died in 2000, as honorary international president of the Mensa Society. I think he did quite well.

Now, let me ask you a question. Did Victor suddenly get smart at thirty years old? Of course not. IQ changes little over time. He was smart the entire time. What changed about Victor was the way he saw himself. He no longer woke up in the morning, looked in the mirror, and saw a stupid idiot. Instead, he saw a genius. What you see is what you get. Once Victor discovered his gold—he was ready to face the world with confidence.

Your Perspective

Here's what I've noticed. You cannot consistently perform in a manner that is inconsistent with the way you see yourself. In the diagram above, the top line represents your potential. It stands for who you really are, what you could really do if you wanted to. The bottom line represents your perspective—your self-image. It stands for who you think you are, what you think you can pull off. Now, notice the jagged line going up and down. This line represents your performance, how you act. You will usually perform at a level that reflects your perspective. If you think you are average, you'll perform in an average way. Once in a while, you may have a really great day, and perform higher than normal. (Notice the line above.) You'll think, *That was awesome. I really outdid myself!* However, most people quickly retreat back to a lower level of living, because they don't think they deserve it. They don't see themselves that way. And they miss their potential. Ouch.

Mr. Sonne is a businessman. When his son Lars was diagnosed with autism as a two-and-a-half-year-old, he didn't expect a career change. But watching his son's disability cause his classmates to bully him, he decided he'd discover the positives about autism. And boy, did he. He now leads an organization that employs people with autism to do IT projects others may not do as well. "There are millions of vacant jobs in IT. Many are well suited for those who are high functioning autistic people," he says. "A lot of people with autism have much to offer but feel rejected or are school dropouts." Some scientists are now challenging our current view of autism as a disability. Author Tyler Cowen believes, "We've had far too much diagnosis and far too little considering what keen, specialized perception…they bring to society. In fact, mainstream society is already reaping the benefits of mimicking autistic cognitive strengths."[i]

The bottom line? Sometimes gold is disguised as garbage. Our influence depends on finding the gold inside.

The Iceberg teaches us that we need to lead ourselves before we lead others. The Starving Baker teaches us we need to feed ourselves before we feed others. The Golden Buddha teaches us we must read ourselves before we read others. Find your gold, and lead from your strengths.

A Look at the Book

Check out two Scriptures in your Bible. The first is Psalm 139:13-15:

> *For You created my innermost being; you knit me together in my mother's womb. I praise You because I am fearfully and wonderfully made; your works are wonderful, I know them full well. My frame was not hidden from you when I was made in the secret place…*

When King David wrote this psalm, he was taking personal inventory of how God had created him and what he put inside. He marveled at God's artistic ability. What does this psalm teach us about our Creator and about our personal value?

It's time for you to take personal inventory. Think about the qualities and abilities God put in you. Take your time. We don't do this enough. Now, list the qualities and abilities you possess:

Qualities (Positive attributes about your personality):

_____

_____

_____

Abilities (Gifts that "add value" to others; things you can do well):

_____

_____

_____

Passions (Desires you have inside that you'd love to pursue in your career or personal life):

_____

_____

_____

Opportunities (Circumstances that present you with a chance to use your potential):

_____

_____

_____

Affirmation (Words of recognition you've received about your potential from others):

Now, check out II Corinthians 5:17-18:

Therefore, if anyone is in Christ, he is a new creation. The old has gone, the new has come. All this is from God, who reconciled us to Himself through Christ and gave us the ministry of reconciliation.

In this Scripture, we are called "new creations." In the original language of the Bible, the term meant "a new species of being that's never existed before." Wow. How should this affect our self-esteem as Christians?

GETTING PERSONAL

Evaluate yourself on the following issues. Circle the one that most honestly describes you.

I tend to overreact when people criticize me:
NEVER   SELDOM   SOMETIMES   OFTEN   CONSISTENTLY

I am often "down" on myself:
NEVER   SELDOM   SOMETIMES   OFTEN   CONSISTENTLY

I feel possessions and beauty are very important:
NEVER   SELDOM   SOMETIMES   OFTEN   CONSISTENTLY

I usually don't work hard, feeling I can't succeed:
NEVER   SELDOM   SOMETIMES   OFTEN   CONSISTENTLY

I am uncomfortable when alone or inactive:
NEVER   SELDOM   SOMETIMES   OFTEN   CONSISTENTLY

I struggle with insecurity, envy, and jealousy:
NEVER   SELDOM   SOMETIMES   OFTEN   CONSISTENTLY

I fear unfamiliar circumstances:
NEVER   SELDOM   SOMETIMES   OFTEN   CONSISTENTLY

My standards of morality are not especially high:
NEVER   SELDOM   SOMETIMES   OFTEN   CONSISTENTLY

PRACTICING THE TRUTH

You've already begun a personal inventory above. Now, here's a challenge for you. Study the books of Ephesians, Galatians, Colossians, I and II Corinthians, jotting down all the "gifts" God has placed inside you now that you are in Christ. Look for the phrases "in Christ," "in Him" and "with Him."

Draw a diagram of a person (you) and list those gifts inside the diagram. Then put this diagram up on your mirror or someplace you'll see it each day. Confess out loud who you are in Christ as you comb your hair and get ready in the morning.

80

78

75

Thermostat and Thermometer

PEOPLE ARE EITHER THERMOMETERS OR THERMOSTATS. THEY WILL MERELY REFLECT THE CLIMATE AROUND THEM, OR THEY WILL SET IT. LEADERS DEVELOP VALUES AND PRINCIPLES TO LIVE BY AND SET THE TONE FOR OTHERS.

You may remember when you first figured out the difference between a thermometer and a thermostat in your home. As a kid, I began to understand it when my science teacher brought it to my attention in the fourth grade. Up until then, I just knew our home had a thermometer hanging outside of our back patio that told us what temperature it was outside. And I knew we had a little box on our living room wall that Mom and Dad would fiddle with when the house got too hot or too cold. I'll never forget when it first dawned on me that, while both had something to do with the temperature, they were fundamentally different. The thermostat set the temperature. The thermometer only reflected what the temperature was.

This is a great picture of another leadership truth. Most people are like thermometers. They tend to reflect the culture around them. They buy things that others buy, say things that others say, wear things that others wear and value things that others value. Oh, there are slight variations. But most people don't set the "climate" for the world they live in. They just mirror back that climate.

Leaders, on the other hand, are people who decide to take life to the next level. They become thermostats, and set the social climate in which they are placed. For instance, you may know people who set the spiritual temperature of a group. They are excited about life and their work. You may know some who determine the attitudes of others by their presence in the room. They're pacesetters. They influence, rather than merely get influenced by people. My challenge to you is to move from being a thermometer to a thermostat.

So, how do we do this? Leaders who are "thermostats" have developed values and principles they live by. God calls us to be authentic. The word "authentic" comes from the root word "to author." It means to write your own story, not copy someone else's. When someone owns a set of values, it's like they have a moral compass on the inside that guides them in their decisions. Dr. Billy Graham is respected today, but not because his preaching is so flashy or insightful. It's because people know him as a man who lives by his values and won't drift from them. People respect others who are values-driven and principle-centered. In fact, leaders like Dr. Billy Graham, Nelson Mandela and Mother Teresa are all like healthy "thermostats." They have two common traits:

1. They live by values (They possess a moral compass)

2. They add value (Their actions serve and help others)

All the leaders I genuinely respect, I respect not because of their title or position. It's because of the life they live. They live by a higher standard, and they are constantly doing things for other people, not themselves.

When leaders fail to develop values, tragedy almost always follows. Athletes who claim to be role models, but who we later learn used illegal drugs or committed crimes, lose their credibility. Again, Lance Armstrong illustrates this. Talk is cheap. He didn't have a skill problem. It was a values problem.

THERMOSTATS BY ACCIDENT

Years ago, a boy grew up in a Jewish home, watching everything his father did. Evidently, his dad didn't realize the influence he had. They attended synagogue until their family moved to another city, and there was no synagogue nearby. Dad decided to just switch religious beliefs. He admitted it was only a way of meeting business contacts anyway. This father's failure to live by values outside of his own benefit led his son to question morality, ethics and his faith. As the boy grew up, he believed that religion was a "crutch" for the masses. He wrote that money was behind anything meaningful in the world. The boy's name was Karl Marx, and he led millions of people into a destructive belief system during the 20th century.

The problem was simple. Karl Marx's father had created a set of values by default, not by design. He didn't think through what was best for his family or his community. He did what was best for himself. Young Karl was a thermometer, reflecting what his dad had modeled. Unfortunately, Karl Marx was successful at making people believe he could be a trusted thermostat.

Regrettably, many leaders do this today. We influence others, but don't have a compass that influences us. These leaders may show up on the news, but when we discover the self-absorbed lifestyle they have or the lack of values in their life, they tend to lose our respect. It's all about them. They may have talent but we wouldn't want to actually "follow" them. Philip Kennicott, culture critic for the *Washington Post,* says Americans have become the "most primitive opportunists." Senator Richard Shelby says that when leaders fail, they are "not contrite, and simply consider the fines and penalties as a means to make the problem go away."[ii] Penalties don't transform a thermometer into a thermostat. It's an inside job.

A Look at the Book

Check out a scripture in Luke 6:46-49. Jesus is speaking and He says:

Why do you call me 'Lord, Lord' and do not do what I say? For everyone who hears these words of mine and acts on them is like a man building a house, who dug deep and laid a foundation on the rock. When the flood rose, the river crashed against that house and couldn't shake it, because it was well built. But the one who hears and does not act is like a man who built his house on the sand. The river crashed against it, and immediately it collapsed. And the destruction of that house was great.

Jesus asked an interesting question: How can we call Him "Lord" but not live by the values He lays out for us? Why is there a gap between what we say and what we do?

What did Jesus say were the differences between the man who built his house on the sand, and the one who built his house on the rock?

_____

_____

_____

What does this story teach us about our values? What is the connection between living like a thermostat and living like a thermometer?

_____

_____

_____

_____

Samantha was six years old when she and her dad were enjoying an amusement park one Saturday. They walked up to a booth where a man was guessing people's weight. A large, heavy-set man stepped up, and the employee attempted to guess his weight. Then, the hefty man stepped on the scale only to find out it was broken. The needle moved only slightly, and the scale reported that the man weighed 25 pounds. At that point, Samantha said to her dad, "Look, Dad! A hollow man."

Hmmm. As people examine our integrity and values, may they never say that about us.

Getting Personal

Take a moment to do an honest evaluation on whether you "act" or "react" more often in life. Are you a thermostat, who acts based on principles and values you embrace, or do you react to situations like a thermometer, reflecting the temperature in the room? Rate yourself honestly below. Assess your life at home, work, school and in the community. Why did you give yourself that evaluation?

I   2   3   4   5   6   7   8   9   I O
<THERMOMETER   THERMOSTAT>

_____

_____

_____

Practicing the Truth

Do you have a set of core values? If not, why not begin a list of your values below. Let me give you some guidelines, before you begin to write:

1. Values can be defined with simple words that describe what you deeply believe.

2. Values are words that describe what you live by or what you want to live by.

3. Values are beliefs that define who you are and are guidelines for your big decisions.

4. Values are stronger than thoughts or opinions. They are ideals of you at your best.

5. Values are the inner-based principles that will fuel the direction of your life.

Think of some words that could be your core values. Write them down, then write a statement of what that word means to you. Then, discuss and explain to your group why you chose your words. (Some people have written nouns like integrity, trusting relationships, or service. Others have chosen adjectives like generous, or caring, or hard-working. It doesn't matter—just be consistent.)

_____

_____

_____

_____

_____

_____

_____

_____

If you're not ready for this exercise, try this challenge. Go find an organization, company or ministry that is working and working well. I believe that if you take the time to push through all the activities, services, programs or products, sooner or later you will come face to face with a person who has no confusion about who they are or what they are about. Write down what you observe about that leader and their values.

_____

_____

_____

_____

_____

_____

_____

_____

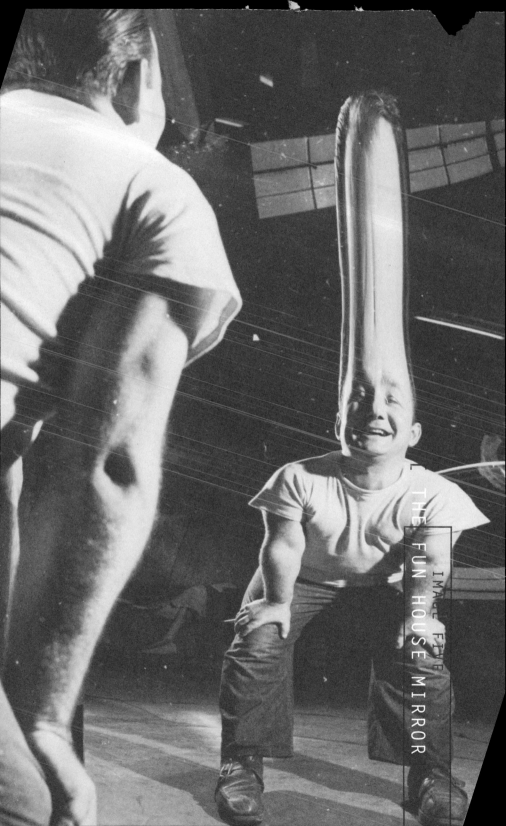

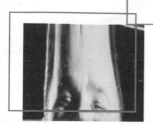

The Fun House Mirror

CARNIVALS OFTEN HAVE MIRRORS THAT DISTORT HOW WE REALLY LOOK. POOR LEADERS DO THIS, PRETENDING OR POSING TO BE BETTER THAN THEY REALLY ARE. OUR LEVEL OF INTEGRITY IS THE TRUE REFLECTION OF WHO WE ARE.

Most carnivals have a fun house somewhere on the premises. Inside the fun house, there is usually a mirror. The mirror isn't flat, so it cannot give you an accurate reflection of what you look like. It is purposefully curved and shaped so it will distort your height or your size in some way. Short folks can look extremely tall; skinny people can look fat—due to the contour of the mirror. It's designed to make you laugh because you end up looking so different than you do in reality. Sadly, this is a picture of a great temptation leaders face: to project a false image of themselves. Sometimes, leaders don't even possess a realistic view of who they are.

Nathan desperately wanted to be elected to the student government at his college. Unfortunately, he knew his chances were slim. He wasn't well known, and tons of popular students were on the election ballot. "Why did so many popular students suddenly run for office?" he wondered.

Two weeks before the election, he grew frantic. He wanted this position badly, and he was willing to pay almost any price to get it. During the mandatory debates between candidates, he feared he would come across as inferior. After all, there was so much talent up there next to him. He was at a crossroads when one of the judges asked him what qualified him to hold office. He was intimidated.

He thought for a moment. Then, he did something he never planned on doing. He lied. It was just a little, white lie. No one would notice. He told his sophomore classmates that he had served as a student government officer before. He paused and looked out at the audience. He had their attention. His answer seemed to please everyone. So he went further. He announced that in high school he raised money to purchase a large flat screen and an Xbox for the school dining hall. Some from the audience applauded. He was on a roll. After a split second of thought, he decided to go for it. He told everyone that before he transferred to the university, he stood up to his community college president and got some of the policies changed.

Each time he ventured out with another white lie, he seemed to gain in stature and popularity. People were finally noticing him. He was somebody. That is, until later, when his friends confronted him on it. They asked him why he had never shared all those things with them before. He started to lie some more, but decided to come clean. He admitted he'd made up most of what he said. He laughed nervously, hoping they would join in. They didn't. He had not only betrayed them, he was pretending to be someone he wasn't. They began to wonder what else he had lied about in his past. Their friendship began to slowly unravel.

This was only the beginning of his trouble. He got enough votes to tie with another student he was running against. Now, it was showdown time with the faculty advisors. He was asked detailed questions about his past experience in student government. He wasn't ready for this. He didn't have an answer. Suspicious that he was making things up, Dr. Rayburn, the Dean of Students, asked to talk with him privately. He asked Nathan how he went about "standing up" to his last president, as he had mentioned in the debate. Dr. Rayburn's eyes were penetrating. Nathan's mouth grew dry. He was out of ideas on how he could wiggle out of this one. He finally confessed that he didn't exactly stand up to his president...and that he'd made up a few things that he shared at the debate. This began a long conversation between the two of them about why Nathan felt he had to lie to win. Slowly, it began to dawn on Nathan that he was now in trouble with his friends, with the entire sophomore class and with the school administration. All because he felt that who he really was—wasn't good enough.

Leadership can be intimidating. Most of us feel that we don't measure up. We have this quiet fear that if people really knew us, they wouldn't want us as their friend, not to mention their leader. George O'Leary was a great football coach at Georgia Tech during the 1990s. When Notre Dame invited him to become their new head coach, things crumbled. For some reason, O'Leary felt he had to distort who he was. He lied about his education to make himself look better. When this was discovered, he lost the job. Unfortunately, when we start to distort our image of who we are, it always comes back to haunt us. The Bible is right again—eventually, your sins will find you out. The damage can be more impactful than the goal you sought. Shortcuts don't pay off in the long run.

You may remember a movie that came out early in 2003 called *Catch Me If You Can*. The film was based on a true story. I read the book years ago. It's the story of Frank Abagnale Jr. and his wild and crazy life as a doctor, airline pilot, banker, investor, attorney and celebrity. The irony behind his story is that he wasn't any of these in reality. He deserves an Academy Award for his portrayal of these professions. He was an intentional fake. A fraud. He was a pretender.

It all began when he realized, as a teen, that he had an uncanny ability to convince people he was "somebody" through his sheer confidence and acting talent. He began to make money at this "game" and soon found himself addicted to role-playing. Before it was over, he'd helped perform surgery in an operating room, conned banks out of thousands of dollars, flown an airplane as a pilot and gone to places most of us only dream of going. The only problem was—it was all a show. It wasn't real. A few years into it, he wanted out. The glamour was gone. He was desperate to come clean, but he had created such a web of deceit, he was stuck. The FBI was on to him, and he ended up spending years in a federal prison. Frank had legitimate talent, but wasted it pretending to be someone else.

The word "integrity" is misunderstood. It simply means to be whole. To be one unit—as in, one integer. When we talk about the integrity of the Scriptures, it means the unified message of the Bible. To have integrity doesn't mean we have perfect character; it means we're not hypocritical. Who we are and what we say are the same. The truth is, people desire authentic leaders. I love the word "authentic." It comes from the term "to author." Authentic leaders author their own life; they don't pose as someone else.

A Look at the Book

Check out the passage in Matthew 23:25:

> Woe to you, scribes and Pharisees, hypocrites! For you cleanse the outside of the cup and dish, but inside you are full of extortion and self-indulgence.

What was Jesus really saying here? When He compared the religious leaders to a cup, what was the distortion He was accusing them of in their leadership?

In Matthew 5:37, Jesus said to "let our 'yes' be 'yes' and our 'no' be 'no.' All else proceeds from evil." In other words, talk straight. Don't swear. Don't exaggerate. Don't get preoccupied with impressing others. Just tell the truth about who you are and what you do. Why is this so difficult for us as leaders?

_____

_____

_____

_____

Who do you know who exhibits integrity? How?

_____

_____

_____

Getting Personal

I believe each of us carries around four images of ourselves. We feel the weight of all four. Three of them are excess baggage. Notice the diagram on the next page. The outer layer represents the image others have of us. The next layer represents the image we project to others. The third layer represents the image we have of ourselves. Finally, the fourth layer represents the truth about who we really are. It is God's image of us, who we really are.

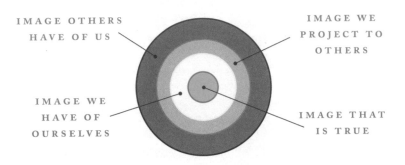

IMAGE OTHERS
HAVE OF US

IMAGE WE
PROJECT TO
OTHERS

IMAGE WE
HAVE OF
OURSELVES

IMAGE THAT
IS TRUE

Assess your own baggage. Which of these four images consumes most of your time? Why?

_____

_____

_____

_____

_____

Practicing the Truth

For one solid week, make a commitment to not lie, exaggerate or distort the truth. In your conversations, speak honestly about yourself. If you accidentally exaggerate something, commit yourself to return to that person and apologize; then, correct the statement you made to reflect the truth. At the end of the week, evaluate how difficult this was. How many times did you have to apologize to someone?

_____

_____

_____

_____

_____

The Oversized Gift

LEADERS ARE OFTEN GIFTED. THEY CAN BEGIN TO DEPEND ON THEIR GIFT FOR SUCCESS, TO THE NEGLECT OF THEIR CHARACTER. THEY BEGIN TO "WING IT." LEADERS SABOTAGE THEMSELVES WHEN THEIR GIFT IS BIGGER THAN THEY ARE.

Imagine you are five years old and your parents throw a birthday party for you. At the party, each of your friends gives you a gift. Afterward, your mom and dad announce they have a couple of special gifts for you out in the garage. You begin to imagine it might be a new bike or a water gun for the pool. When you dart out to see them, you are shocked. You guessed correctly, but it is so much more. In front of you are a twelve-gauge shotgun and a huge Harley-Davidson motorcycle!

You wouldn't believe your eyes, would you? How cool is this! But after a second thought, wouldn't you wonder about your mom and dad's sanity? You're only five years old! Shotguns and motorcycles are great—but they are for adults. You really need to mature a little bit before you'd be ready for them. In fact, although you may want to try out the gifts, you could endanger many lives, including your own, if you did. The gifts just don't fit the person.

This is a picture of many talented people on earth today. God has given them large gifts, or talents and abilities. Some can speak really well. Some can organize programs. Some can sing or play the guitar or keyboard. Some have gifts in graphic design. However, when people lean on the gifts God gave them and fail to mature emotionally or spiritually, they may ruin their chance to use the gift as God designed. The gift is bigger than they are. If their character has not kept up with their talent, they learn to "wing it" through life, depending on their gift rather than on God or their character. This choice to "wing it" can result in a loss of trust. In short, it's the classic story of the kid who is so good on the stage—but so horrible off the stage.

Michael Jackson's legacy will live for decades. He became a pop star when he was only five years old. He had amazing talent. He could sing. He could dance. He could produce music videos like no one else. During the '70s, '80s and '90s he was one of the most-talked-about celebrities on the planet. Unfortunately, he never experienced a normal life. In some ways, he never matured. He didn't connect with other kids his own age when he was young. He was always on stage or in a recording studio. His gift thrust him there. Emotionally, he was up and down. Part of his legacy is heartbreaking. Although he was the King of Pop, he was questioned on TV because he liked to hang around kids all the time. In the end, he was charged with several counts of sexually abusing children. Although he settled out of court, the story was mixed and sad.

What was the problem between his professional life and his personal life? His gift was bigger than he was. His talent matured, but it was at the expense of his integrity. He struggled with growing in the other areas of his life because so much attention was given to his talent. It was an oversized gift.

We see this "oversized gift" every week in the news. It takes the form of an NCAA athlete who is a great wide receiver or strong forward, but who keeps making bad decisions off the field—and eventually gets kicked off the team or, worse, arrested for a crime. It's as though the player assumes they're invincible. We all ask, How could such a talented person do such a stupid thing? Their gift blinded them from seeing reality.

It can also take the form of a young actor or actress, like Lindsay Lohan, who broke into the entertainment world as a child model when she was three years old. At 11, she starred in Disney's remake of the movie *The Parent Trap*. She was adorable. Sadly, the rest of her life fell apart. She's been in and out of court, spent time in jail, and fought addictive behaviors through her teens and twenties. Now consider Whitney Houston's incredible voice. Although she sold 200 million records in her lifetime, she died with a $20 million debt. Her story ended sadly—due to addictions. My explanation? Her gift was huge. Her life didn't keep up. It was an oversized gift. It's people of influence who are great in front of the camera…but not so much with the rest of their lives.

It can take the form of Olympic athletes or baseball players like Ryan Braun or Alex Rodriguez who sacrifice their body, personal life, and the rest of their career and reputation, for a few years playing a game on steroids. The performance-enhancing drug may help them today, but the rest of their life has been sabotaged. Short-term benefit. Long-term consequence.

Are Talents Bad?

So what am I saying? Are big talents bad? Not at all. We love to see people with God-given talent perform or lead. But often the inner life is left underdeveloped due to the spotlight on the outer life. We're distracted by the gift. Charisma becomes mammoth. Character becomes minimized. The solution is not to do away with talent; it is to give attention to developing our discipline and personality. Our inward character is the infrastructure that holds us up through our lives. And you can't "wing it" in building discipline. I believe the greater the size of your gifts, the more time you must dedicate to developing your personal, inner life.

There's a great story about a millionaire who asked a builder to construct a house. He showed him the blueprints, then gave him a huge amount of money. The millionaire told the builder, "You probably won't need all this money, but I want you to have plenty to build a solid house. When you are finished, you can keep whatever money you have left over."

The builder smiled. Inside, he thought: I can build a house for a fraction of this money. Then, I can pocket most of the money for myself! So he did. He began to throw that house together quickly. He put studs five feet apart; he pounded only one nail per board; he slapped on one, thin coat of paint. He threw on the shingles and barely covered the roof of the house. Later, when he was finished, he knew the house wasn't solid, but at least it looked good, and he had lots of money left over. He returned to the millionaire and said, "Here are the keys to the house." In that moment, the millionaire smiled and responded: "Oh, I forgot to tell you...the house is yours."

That poor builder had no idea he was building his own house. Does this sound familiar? I believe there are times God looks at us and says, "Do you realize the life you're building is your life?" You can take shortcuts, but you will only hurt yourself. You can misuse your talent and try to project an image for your peers—but eventually the inside truth about you will come out.

A Look at the Book

Check out Psalm 15:1-2. It says:

> O Lord, who may abide in Your tent? Who may dwell in Your holy hill? He who walks with integrity, and works righteousness, and speaks truth in his heart.

In this psalm, David asks the question: Who can spend time in God's presence? Who is able to be intimate with God? The answer: People with integrity, who do right and are truthful. Notice he said nothing about having lots of talent or being very smart. What does this tell us about God?

_____

_____

_____

God desires us to be authentic Christians. Let me remind you that the word "authentic" comes from the Greek word meaning "to author." To be authentic means to author your own life. You don't pretend or "wing it" or copy someone else. You take initiative to make it good. On a scale of one to ten, how well do you author your own life? Discuss your answer.

1	2	3	4	5	6	7	8	9	10

< I WING IT   I BUILD MY LIFE ON PURPOSE >

Proverbs 18:16 tells us: *A man's gift makes room for him and brings him before great men.* Obviously, our gifts and talents can get us somewhere. But our character will keep us there. How much do you lean on your "gifts" rather than your character?

_____

_____

_____

GETTING PERSONAL

Take a minute and think about your "gifts" and your character. Gifts are often things people can see, but character is invisible at first. (People have to look closer to see it.) Compare your gifts to the outside of a house and your character to the inside of the house. List your top three gifts below:

1. _____
2. _____
3. _____

Now, list your top three character qualities that strengthen you on the inside. It may be discipline, or honesty, or listening skills, or compassion, etc.:

1. _____
2. _____
3. _____

Now, honestly evaluate your life: which of these lists do you rely on to keep your life together? Which do you spend more time developing? Which is more impressive to other people?

_____

_____

_____

PRACTICING THE TRUTH

Select a leader in your community that you believe is talented, and who exhibits integrity and character. Set up an interview with them, and find out how they developed these leadership qualities. Talk about both talent and character and what role both of these played. Discuss these questions:

1. What gifts do you have that helped you get to the top?

_____

_____

2. What role did discipline play in your life?

_____

_____

_____

3. How important was your integrity?

_____

_____

_____

4. Did you ever have a time when you failed in your career? How did it happen?

_____

_____

_____

5. What advice would you give me about my gifts and my character?

_____

_____

_____

IMAGE SEVEN
[PERSONAL LAPTOP]

Personal Laptop

OUR MINDS WORK LIKE A COMPUTER. THEY ONLY SPIT OUT THE DATA THEY HAVE BEEN FED. GARBAGE IN, GARBAGE OUT. LEADERS ARE DISCIPLINED ABOUT WHAT THEY STORE IN THEIR MIND AND HEART.

Chances are, you use a computer. You may own one yourself. It's hard to imagine living life without one these days. Computers can be your best friend or your worst enemy. They are wonderful when they've been given the right information. When you store data inside the hard drive, you have it forever. You can file it away and forget about it. It's yours. And you can call it up whenever you need it. Phone numbers. Email addresses. Documents for work. Your computer can give you access to the internet where you can retrieve information and do instant messaging with friends and colleagues. It's all there at your fingertips.

Unfortunately, your computer can be your enemy. It depends on what you've done with it. When you go to locate a paper you need for a meeting—you won't find it unless you stored it there. Duh! It only stores the information you actually save on it. The Internet, with all its valuable information, can also be a disaster. Garbage can be found on it, like pornography, that will keep coming back over and over again. Once you call it up—watch out. You will be haunted by it for months to come.

Here's the principle. Our minds work like sophisticated computers. They are laptops with great memory. They are small and portable. Along the way, you store information in them. People you meet. Stuff you read. Pictures you see. Good or bad.

That's why leaders are disciplined about what they store in their mind and heart. They don't feed on garbage, because they know the GIGO principle: garbage in, garbage out. Leaders work hard at investing the right material inside themselves. They also work hard avoiding the wrong material, so that what comes out—is right. It was the late Dr. Hans Selye who popularized the fact that every human being has a tiny membrane in the back of their head. It is called RAS: Reticular Activating System. This membrane has a primary function: to cause you to move in the direction of the dominant thought of the moment. As humans, we naturally act on the stuff that fills our minds. We become preoccupied with thoughts and eventually want to act on those thoughts. Hmmm. Maybe this explains a lot of things. Maybe it explains why so many rapes happen after guys have watched pornography night after night. Maybe it explains the huge amount of violence among people between the ages of 12 and 24. The average kid has seen more than 4,000 murders on TV during that time,[iii] not to mention in video games. The Indiana University School of Medicine has studied how the images we see impact our brains. For instance, normal adolescents who had a higher level of exposure to violence in the media had reduced levels of cognitive function.[iv] In other words, the more violence they saw, the less thinking, learning, reasoning and emotional stamina they have. The garbage they fed into their minds has affected what's coming out. Their little laptop computer inside has stored the wrong information— and now they can only retrieve the wrong stuff.

Some may say they don't agree. They don't believe that what we see and hear affects our behavior. If that were true, however, no company would ever advertise on TV again. It does affect us. I have to chuckle when I see a movie preview and hear a voiceover say "For mature audiences only." Why? This principle doesn't favor kids or adults. We all have laptops inside of us. In fact, another analogy for our mind is a bank account. Our minds and hearts are like a checking account at a local bank. We can only withdraw what we've deposited. It doesn't matter if you think you are mature or not. What matters is, what did you put in the account?

So what does it look like for a leader to practice this truth? Consider Barrett Jones, former team captain for the University of Alabama football team, who was drafted in 2013 by the St. Louis Rams. At Alabama, he was an All-American at three positions and a starter for four years. The team won three national championships while Jones was there. On top of his athletic achievements, Jones volunteered in Haiti after its 2010 earthquake and helped clear away debris in Tuscaloosa, Alabama, after tornadoes there. All the while, he was earning all A's, a bachelor's degree, and a master's degree—in four and a half years.

"Some people feel like they have to be good at school, and they really stress about it," Jones says. "I never really stressed about it. I just kind of did it. I have a desire to be excellent at everything I do."

How does Barrett live this way? He is careful to feed his mind well. I spoke to him and heard how disciplined he is in what he reads, listens to and watches. He knows his mind is a personal laptop. Because of this discipline, he's won the respect of coaches and teammates. Coach Nick Saban not only considers Jones one of the five best players he's ever coached, but also one of the "top people in the history of college football." Saban even went so far as to say Jones is one of the five most influential people in his own life.

"I think Barrett has just a genuine, great character about him," Saban says. "He has great thoughts, habits, priorities. He's compassionate. He's willing to serve other people. The team is important to him; he's positive. He's responsible. He's a very hard worker. It's so rare to find a combination of all those things in one person."[v]

WHO ARE YOU FEEDING?

Maybe the truth of this chapter can be summed up in a story. I once heard of a teenage girl who lived in Alaska. She was struggling with her faith as a Christian. Part of her wanted to do what was right and follow Christ. Another part of her was still rebellious. One day, she went to see her youth pastor. She described her dilemma this way. She said it was like there were two husky dogs inside of her fighting all the time—one good and one bad. She felt the pull of these forces all day. These "dogs" were constantly struggling to control her. Finally, her youth pastor asked, "Which of the two dogs is stronger?"

She thought for a moment. Then, it was like a light bulb went on inside of her. She said, "I guess whichever dog I feed the most."

Bingo. Leaders are disciplined about what they store inside their mind and heart. They listen to positive input—great speakers, helpful content and encouraging music. They fill themselves with Scripture. They are cautious about content that will hinder or confuse their decision-making ability later. And their laptop inside affects the respect they get from others. What we are filled with does spill out. Do you want to make an impact with your life in the future? You will become what you are becoming right now. What are you feeding your mind and heart today?

A LOOK AT THE BOOK

Check out Proverbs 4:20-25:

> My son, give attention to my words; incline your ear to my teachings. Do not let them depart from your sight; keep them in the midst of your heart. For they are life to those who find them, and health to their whole body. Watch over your heart with all diligence, for from it flow the springs of life… Let your eyes look directly ahead, and let your gaze be fixed straight in front of you.

This proverb tells us to guard our hearts and minds. What is the reason for this?

_____

_____

_____

Why do you think this passage puts such an emphasis on what is deposited inside of us?

_____

_____

_____

Why is following this instruction so difficult today? How can you improve on guarding your heart?

_____

_____

_____

Getting Personal

Romans 10:17 tells us that "faith comes by hearing—hearing the word of God." We grow in faith by consuming more and more of the Word of God, in a trusting heart. How much do you consume God's Word each week?

_____

_____

_____

Think about all the "input" you receive into your mental "laptop" each week. List the positive and the negative input you store away inside of you, from TV shows, to music, to material you read, to people you talk to, to things you see on the internet, etc. Make a log of the good and bad you take in below:

NEGATIVE INPUT	POSITIVE INPUT
_____	_____
_____	_____
_____	_____
_____	_____
_____	_____
_____	_____

Do you believe you are feeding the right "husky dog" inside you enough?

_____

_____

Practicing the Truth

Watch TV some evening, or see a movie (with family or friends) in which you know one of the characters has questionable values. Watch the program or movie with the purpose of discussing the content afterward. When it is over, discuss how often you heard lies on the TV commercials, the program or the movie. (For example, how did the commercials over-promise what they can deliver?) Did you hear any outright lies? How did the characters in the movie display unhealthy values? Were they deceitful? If so, why were they?

_____

_____

_____

Next, talk about the input you received. How do we become numb to this input over time? Contrast what you saw with principles or truths from Scripture. Can you think of a truth that counters the input you received that night? Focus on the positive value or truth. Then, talk about Romans 12:2:

_____

_____

_____

Don't be conformed to this world, but be transformed by the renewing of your mind... What does this mean?

_____

_____

_____

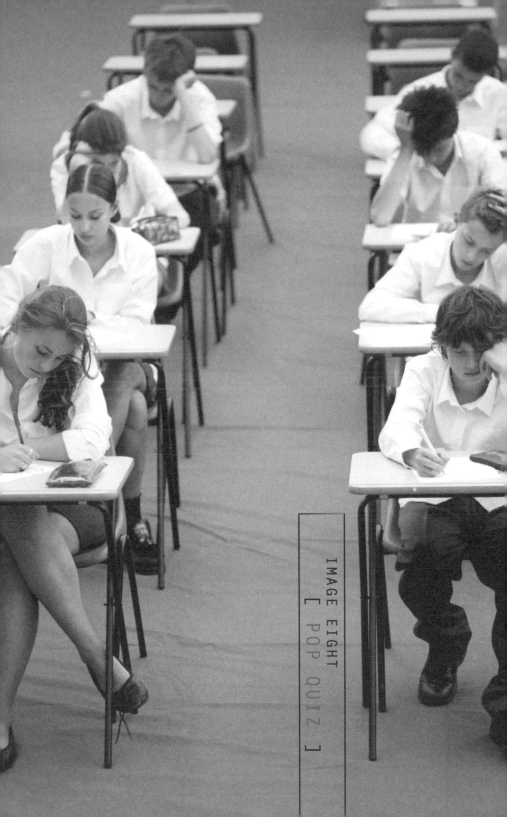

IMAGE EIGHT
[POP QUIZ]

Pop Quiz

LEADERS EXPERIENCE TESTS AS THEY MATURE. THESE TESTS RANGE FROM MOTIVE CHECKS, TO AUTHORITY TESTS, TO INTEGRITY CHECKS. THEY REVEAL THE LEADER'S POTENTIAL AND MATURITY, AND ARE A PATHWAY TO PROGRESS.

Few students around the world actually enjoy taking tests. In school, examinations are usually met with a negative attitude. Ugh! Most students hate them. However, tests are used consistently by teachers to enable students to demonstrate what they've learned. I had a Spanish teacher who hated giving tests to her classes. She was a sweet grandmother type, who loved every one of her students. And she loved teaching. Tests were the only negative part of the deal for her. She gave us a pop quiz every week at some point, but would always say the same thing before handing out the tests: "I wish I didn't have to give you this test, but it is the only way we're going to know whether you are ready to move on to the next section in the course."

She was right. Tests are no fun, but they are necessary. They are measuring sticks. Checkpoints. Places to evaluate. It's true for leaders as well. I have noticed through the last thirty years of my life that leaders all experience tests at each state of their growth. Tests are opportunities that challenge us to prove our potential and maturity. Let me offer a few truths I have observed about the tests that leaders endure:

1. We all experience tests at each stage of our growth.
   No one is exempt from the leadership tests that come with leadership responsibility.
2. Our goal in every case should be to pass the test.
   We should anticipate them and assume a positive outlook on how we can pass each test.
3. Testing always precedes promotion.
   With every step forward comes some internal preparation that reveals your readiness.
4. Self-promotion and human promotion can never replace divine promotion.
   When we promote ourselves, it does not substitute for true promotion from our leaders.
5. Just as a product is never used until it is tested, so it is with us.
   If we want to be useful or take on greater authority, we can expect great testing en route.

I believe God has the same attitude my Spanish teacher had years ago. He doesn't enjoy seeing His children struggle through life's tests and trials. However, if He were to visit us in person, He would probably say, "I don't enjoy making you go through this, but it is the only way you can prove you are ready for what's ahead. Before I can use you greatly—I must test you deeply."

I really believe the statements above. Each challenge is a stepping stone for new ones that lie ahead. All of life is a preparation for the future. And most of the time, these tests surface without warning, demonstrating what we're really made of. Case in point: Do you remember the earthquake and tsunami that hit Japan in 2011? In the months afterward, Japanese officials reported that $78 million in cash was turned in to the government since the twin-punch earthquake and tsunami hit the country. $48 million was recovered from the wallets and purses found in debris; the other $30 million was in safes, full of cash and gold bars, many of which floated in from the ocean.[vi] What a commentary on the honesty of those people. They passed a test.

Let me offer a list of some of the tests you will experience on your leadership journey:

THE TEST OF SMALL THINGS (LUKE 16:10, EPHESIANS 5:16)
This test comes when we are asked to do something beneath our potential and talent. It proves how faithful we are to commitments and whether we are ready for greater opportunities.

THE MOTIVE CHECK (MATTHEW 6:5-6, JOB 1:9-11)
This test comes to the one who is doing what is right, to reveal their true motive. Why we do something will ultimately determine *what* we do.

THE STEWARDSHIP TEST (LUKE 12:16-21, MATTHEW 25:21)
This test comes to demonstrate how wisely and generously we are handling the resources we have been given. Often we wish we had more or different resources. God says: Use what you have.

THE WILDERNESS TEST (DEUTERONOMY 8:15-16, PSALM 42:1-2)
This test comes when we feel spiritually dry, as if we're in a desert. It reveals our potential to change and enter a new level of growth. It proves we are able to perform even when life isn't fun.

THE CREDIBILITY CHECK (I SAMUEL 16:7, GALATIANS 2:11-14)
This test comes to demonstrate both our ability to get the job done and our personal integrity. It reveals whether we're willing to compromise ethics under pressure.

THE AUTHORITY TEST (I SAMUEL 24:4-20, GALATIANS 2:1-9)
This test comes to reveal our attitude and willing submission to God-given authority, even when we disagree. Before we can be good leaders, we must learn to be good followers.

The Offense Test (Hebrews 12:14-15, Mark 11:25-26)

This test examines how we act when we become offended. Everyone's vulnerable, but leaders are more likely to get criticized since they're up front. The test is about how quickly we forgive others.

The Warfare Test (Exodus 13:17, Jeremiah 12:5)

This test demonstrates our ability to continue in God's vision while experiencing adversity and opposition. Do we give up and decide God must not want us to continue, or do we stick with it?

The Test of Time (Esther 4:14, Galatians 6:9)

This test is twofold: First, it reveals the quality of our work—will it stand over time? Second, it reveals our ability to seize opportunities when they come our way.

The Lordship Test (Luke 5:4-7, Joshua 1:8)

This test reveals our heart response to who or what has the final authority in our lives. When life gets tough—whose voice determines what we will do?

Taking the Tests: Tombstone or Stepping Stone

Over the years I've experienced every one of these tests. They came in subtle moments when I had the chance to keep some petty cash from the cash register at work, or when I got criticized by those on my team, or when I was tempted to quit because I had to make a tough decision. Later, they came in the form of the need to confront a colleague, or downsize staff. I soon learned that tests usually come at critical points through an event or a person. Further, I recognized that how I responded to each test either became a tombstone or a stepping stone for my growth.

Tests are friends, not enemies. Tests communicate all kinds of information about who we really are. How we handle them makes them a positive or negative experience. The life you live daily will determine how ready you are to face leadership tests.

Generally these tests are about my character. And like a good actor in a stage play that doesn't go according to the script—my job is to stay in character! Regardless of what anyone else does—we are to follow our script: the Bible.

A Look at the Book

Check out Genesis 22:1-2. The passage says that God "tested" Abraham. Read the rest of the story. Using the list above, what kind of test do you think God gave Abraham with his son Isaac?

_____

_____

Look up these passages from the Psalms: Psalm 7:9, 17:3, and 26:2. What do these Scriptures communicate to you about testing?

_____

_____

Why do you suppose we avoid tests in life whenever possible? What makes it difficult to see the benefits of tests in our lives?

_____

_____

Getting Personal

Take a moment and review the list of tests above. Which of these tests have you experienced recently? How did you do in response to it, on a scale of one to ten?

1	2	3	4	5	6	7	8	9	10
<FAILED THE TEST						PASSED THE TEST>			

As you think about a specific test you have experienced over the last year, reflect on how well you responded to it. I have found that "tests" in my life reveal one of three things:

1. Inward Poverty – I did worse than I have in the past

2. Inward Plateau – I responded the same as I have in the past

3. Inward Progress – I have grown in my life, based on how I responded

Based on your response to the test, do you see inward poverty, plateau or progress in that area?

Practicing the Truth

Here's a fun assignment. Go to the shopping mall with a group of friends or colleagues. As you window-shop, secretly drop a $20 bill on the floor, where they will see it. Make sure they do not know you are the source of the money. When one of them spots it, act as though you don't know where it came from. Don't offer any suggestions to them on what to do. Allow them to reveal their heart. Do your comrades think they should keep it? Do they disagree on what to do? Does anyone from the group suggest that they try to find the owner? Does someone suggest that everyone else would just keep it, so why shouldn't they? Within a few minutes, you should be ready to discuss what to do with your find.

Once everyone draws a conclusion, talk about how it reflects the personal values they've embraced. Talk about how these kinds of situations are like a "test" of our character.

IMAGE NINE
[EMOTIONAL FUEL]

Emotional Fuel

A LEADER'S FUTURE IS SHAPED BY THE PEOPLE CLOSEST TO HIM OR HER. A LEADER'S PERSONAL NETWORK IS HIS EMOTIONAL FUEL: HIS MODELS, HEROES, MENTORS, INNER CIRCLE, AND ACCOUNTABILITY PARTNERS.

Over the years, I have been guilty of driving my car on empty. I try to eke out the last drop of gasoline before stopping at a service station to refuel. I don't know why. Maybe it's because I think it's better stewardship of my time to wait until it is totally drained. Whatever the reason, I have learned in time the dangers of driving on empty. One Sunday morning, my wife and I were driving to church...and the tank was on empty again. She warned me we should stop and get gas. I refused. I was sure I had enough to get to church and back again. I had done it a hundred times before. I could do it again.

Well, you probably know the rest of the story. We ran out of gas. Or, I should say, I ran out of gas. My wife did not want to be associated with this failure. I had to push that car quite a ways to get to the nearest exit and fill the tank. She was smiling when it was all over. I was not.

Cars just don't run well without fuel. In fact, they don't run at all. If you continue to force a car to operate without fuel or oil or transmission fluid for that matter, you are going to run into problems. Automobiles need these fluids to run.

YOUR FUEL IS ALL AROUND YOU

In the same way, leaders run on fuel as well. We need spiritual fuel and emotional fuel. Because leaders spend themselves more than the average person, they need to refuel more often than most people do. Leadership is more emotionally expensive than friendship. In this chapter, I want to talk about the emotional fuel that leaders require. A leader's personal network is his or her emotional fuel. Leaders need people in their lives who don't take from them, but who replenish them. If they don't have this network of people in place, they will use their followers to meet this need. This almost always leads to unhealthy situations.

For instance, some people lead because they are needy. Their emotional tank is empty and they need their followers to fill them up. Obviously, we all need others in our lives for social reasons. But I am talking about an unhealthy leader who uses people to meet his or her need for flattery, prestige or ego fulfillment. Perhaps the leader's self-image rides on whether people like him or her. Let's face it—just having followers can stroke our egos. Some people lead because they are lonely. Not good. Some lead because they need encouragement. If you need people for this, you cannot lead them well. Your perspective will be skewed by your own needs rather than what is best for your organization or team. Leaders must make sure their emotional tank is full before they lead others. Never lead out of need.

When I was a student I worked for a man who led from an empty tank. In fact, he confided in me that he was intimidated by the people and board members in the organization. I was stunned to hear this because this leader seemed so together. He confessed to me he had a poor self-image and wasn't secure or confident in his decisions. He had no accountability and no mentors. The result? During the next four years, that organization fell apart. It unraveled in front of my eyes—not because we didn't have sufficient funds or a good strategy. It was because the leader was running on an empty tank. He became consumed by his own needs instead of looking out for the needs of the organization. People began arguing over the direction and the vision, and who was in charge. The team was divided. The leader was eventually asked by the board chairman to leave.

YOUR NETWORK

It has been said that your network determines your net worth. In other words, your value to any team or organization depends on how strong and healthy you are inside. You need to run on all eight cylinders. And your strength depends on your running on a full emotional tank. Our character and our relationships are closely linked. Whenever there is a problem in our character, we pay a price in our relationships. Whenever we have a relationship problem, it affects our character.

Look at the diagram below. Each category represents a set of relationships that will fill your tank and keep you healthy. Take a moment and put the names of people who fit each category for you. Be honest. If you don't have people for each category, think about and discuss why you don't.

MODELS
People who do what
you'd like to do.

_____

_____

HEROES
People you look up
to and admire.

MENTORS
People who coach you
and invest in you.

_____

_____

ME

PARTNERS
Peers who travel with you
and hold you accountable.

INNER CIRCLE
Those who are closest to
you; they're like family.

_____

_____

MENTEES
People who learn from you.

_____

_____

_____

A LOOK AT THE BOOK

Check out Proverbs 27:17:

> *As iron sharpens iron, so one man sharpens another.*

List ways one person can sharpen another person in a relationship.

_____

_____

_____

Check out Proverbs 11:14:

> *Where there is no guidance, the people fall, but in the abundance of counselors
> there is victory.*

Why is it easier to fall without the counsel of others in your life?

_____

_____

_____

Why do you think we need accountability and support in our lives as leaders?

_____

_____

_____

GETTING PERSONAL

Evaluate your answers to the "Your Network" diagram above. Do you have a good balance of relationships that can be your emotional fuel? Which categories do you still need people to fill in your life: models, heroes, mentors, partners, inner circle or followers? Jot down the names of people you can challenge to be part of your network. List what role they can best fill for you.

_____

_____

_____

_____

_____

PRACTICING THE TRUTH

When you conclude what people you still need to make up your network, go and meet with them. Challenge them to play a key role in your network. Invite them to play a bigger role, as a mentor, or partner, or model, or hero or inner circle. Set times to meet with these people at least once a month for support, accountability, encouragement and direction. Invite them to ask these questions of you:

1. What are the goals you are working toward right now?

2. How can I offer direction?

3. In what ways can I hold you accountable?

4. What are your greatest needs? Temptations? Weaknesses?

5. What action step can you take this week? When will you take it?

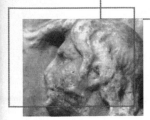

Opportunity Statue

LEADERS MANAGE OPPORTUNITIES. EVERYONE HAS 86,400 SECONDS EACH DAY TO
USE OR ABUSE. OPPORTUNITY IS A STATUE WITH HAIR IN FRONT, BUT BALD IN THE
BACK—YOU CAN'T GRAB IT ONCE IT IS GONE.

In ancient Greece, there were statues everywhere. One man who lived in Athens
centuries ago wrote there were more statues than people at one point. If you were
to walk into Athens, you were sure to see one statue in particular. It was a statue
called "Opportunity." It was a vivid illustration of how opportunity works in our
lives. It was a statue of a person who had long, flowing hair in front of their face—
but was completely bald in back. Weird...but revealing. To put it simply, you could
grab it when it was coming toward you, but you could never get hold of it once it
had passed.

That's how opportunity works. Time is fleeting. You never get it back once it is
gone. Someone said to me recently, "Time is more valuable than money. You can
always get more money, but you can't get more time." Leaders understand this
truth, and they manage their time wisely. They recognize that everyone gets the
same amount of minutes each day—but not everyone makes something out of
those minutes. Let me ask you a question. What if I told you that someone
anonymously deposits some money into your bank account every day. Each day
it is the same amount: 86,400 pennies (which amounts to $864). It is yours to spend
however you wish—but there's just one catch. You have to use it or you will lose
it. Any amount still in the account at midnight each night will be taken away. Here's
my question: how would you spend that money?

I bet you'd think long and hard about how you would spend it. You might even start
making a list of how you would spend it—what you would buy, how much you'd
spend, when and where. Why would you take it so seriously? Simple. Because that's
a pretty good amount of money and you don't want to waste any by the end of the
day. Bingo. That's how we need to treat our time.

I have some good news and bad news. The bad news is, no one is depositing that much money in your bank account. Sorry about that. However, each day, God gives you 86,400 seconds to spend, invest, or waste. But most people don't look at it as anything.

When I was a student in college, I learned a valuable lesson from an unlikely place. I was stressed from a heavy class schedule, trying to hold down two jobs, as well as working with a youth ministry. In addition, I was playing on our dorm intramural basketball team. I felt like I was trying to perform seventeen activities at the same time!

During that year, one of the ministries I joined was a prison outreach to a maximum-security prison in town. It was there I learned this amazing lesson in time management and seizing opportunities. It came from an unlikely person...Joe, one of the inmates. Joe was in for manslaughter. He was serving several years of a prison sentence. He would be in prison for much of the rest of his life. But Joe had become a Christian in prison. While all the other inmates were playing cards or watching TV late one night, Joe was reading a theology book by Martin Luther, the great reformer from the 16th century. He was making notes on a notepad from his reading. I learned he spent most of his days doing this.

Why was he so intent on this activity? He was studying to go into the ministry. I was a bit shocked at his intensity, so I asked him why he didn't take a break and watch TV or play cards with the other inmates. He simply responded with a smile: "You can waste a lot of time with cards or TV."

Waste a lot of time? How could this prisoner say such a thing? Time was all he had—and he had lots of it. He might be in prison the rest of his life! I couldn't believe it, so I asked him how he gained such a perspective. He told me he had read the Scripture in Psalm 90:12: "Teach us to number our days, O Lord, that we may apply our hearts with wisdom." He told me he was just trying to use his time most wisely. His goal was not to stay busy or pass the time with entertainment. It was to be productive. He told me he would either use what he learned when he got out and became a minister, or he'd use it in heaven when he met the Lord face to face. He said the prison had become a great opportunity to prepare himself for the future.

I've never forgotten Joe and the little lesson he taught me. In the New Testament, there are two words to describe time. "Kronos" means time measured on the clock. "Kairos" means opportunity. I've noticed people are always looking for more "kronos." Instead, we need to look for more "kairos" within the "kronos" God has already given us. How can we make the most of what we have? I have the ability to waste lots of time doing things that don't matter. Sometimes I confuse activity with accomplishment. I think staying busy is the goal. And when I take a break from the busy-ness, I tend to "amuse myself to death" with entertainment. But busy-ness or amusement isn't the goal in life. It is doing what counts, one activity at a time.

So How do we do This?

Let me suggest some simple steps you can use to begin seizing the day and doing what counts:

1. Make a "to do" list at the end of each day, for tomorrow.
2. From that list, set your priorities. Label each activity A, B, or C, based on its importance.
3. Question everything. Ask yourself: Is doing this really important?
4. Avoid clutter. Have a place you put everything. Keep it simple.
5. Do things with excellence, but avoid perfectionism.
6. Use a calendar. It will help you see the big picture of where you are going.
7. Think about your long-term goals: How does doing each activity fit with your purpose?

In a poor, remote village in Paraguay, something beautiful has happened. Some of the villagers rummaged through the trash heaped up in the dump, to see if there was anything useful in it. They happened upon a piece of metal that looked like a violin. One of the men took it and began to actually create a violin from the piece of trash. A young girl now plays it. Next, they made a cello, then a horn, and later a flute. This village now has an incredible children's orchestra called "Landfill Harmonic," which performs at a nearly professional level…all because one man's trash became another man's treasure. The man who crafted the first violin seized the opportunity. So did the kids…and their lives have been transformed.

What are you doing with your opportunity?

A Look at the Book

Check out Ephesians 5:15-16:

> *Therefore, be careful how you live, not as unwise men but as wise, making the most of your time, because the days are evil.*

List one way you "make the most of your time" each day.

_____

Finish this sentence: Last year, I never had enough time to

_____

Was your answer something important? Was it something God wanted you to do?

_____

_____

The Scripture says the reason we should be wise with our time is because the "days are evil." What does this have to do with time management?

_____

_____

_____

Why do you think so many of us simply waste so much of our time? Why don't we value it?

_____

_____

_____

Getting Personal

Think about the activities you participate in each week. Now, list the activities under the following three categories. The activities you should give the most time to are the ones that fit into one of these three. You should really focus on any that fall into all three categories!

REQUIRED: The activities you do because you have to; they are required of you by someone.

_____

_____

RESULTS: The activities you do because you are really good at them; they produce results.

_____

_____

REWARD: The activities you do because you enjoy them deeply; they are fulfilling to you.

_____

_____

Practicing the Truth

Prioritize and practice those activities that fit into the categories above. If you have several of them, make a "to do" list now. List the top ten activities of your week and rank them, from the most important one to the least important, in order. The 80/20 Principle teaches us that with the right priorities, the top 20% of your activities gives you 80% of the results you desire. (More about this in book three.) Start living by this set of priorities. Does this sound too strict? You must learn to value your time.

To realize the value of one year, ask a student who has failed his final exam.

To realize the value of one month, ask a mother who just gave birth to a premature baby.

To realize the value of one week, ask the editor of a weekly newspaper.

To realize the value of one day, ask the day laborer who has ten kids to feed.

To realize the value of one hour, ask a boyfriend and girlfriend who are waiting to meet.

To realize the value of one minute, ask the person who just missed his flight.

To realize the value of one second, ask the person who survived a car accident.

To realize the value of one millisecond, ask the person who has won a gold medal.

IMAGE ELEVEN

[DISCIPLINE BRIDGE]

Discipline Bridge

LEADERS DON'T BUILD CHARACTER WITHOUT CROSSING THE BRIDGE OF DISCIPLINE. PERSONAL DISCIPLINE IS LIKE A BRIDGE THAT CROSSES FROM WHERE YOU ARE TO WHERE YOU WANT TO BE. IT GETS YOU WHERE YOU WANT TO GO.

As a boy growing up in Cincinnati, Ohio, my scariest moment happened when a fierce tornado ripped through our little suburban neighborhood. My mom and dad demanded we rush down to the basement—where I immediately discovered how to pray passionately. The wind howled and the rain poured down. We watched debris fly across our backyard from our small basement windows. Bicycles, patio grills, lawn chairs. I even remember seeing a boat take flight. The rain was so heavy it caused flooding in the streets everywhere. It was the worst natural disaster that little town had seen in decades.

Over the next week rescue workers were everywhere attempting to restore what had been demolished. One particular scene sticks in my memory. It was a building that had caved in, and desperately needed repair. However, the rain had flooded the property, making it impossible for workers to get to it on foot. Interestingly, they built a bridge to the damaged building in order to repair it. I remember seeing scores of little bridges in these disaster areas. The bridges enabled the workers to get from where they were to where they wanted to go, and fix the damage.

What a fitting analogy for leaders. Many times, our own character has caved in. It could be due to a disaster—our own personal tornado. Symptoms of the damage may be subtle. Maybe we lost a friendship. It may be financial debt, failing grades or some weight we need to take off. It might even be anxiety or emotional depression. Inside, we feel like we're crumbling—caving in. We need help.

Here's what I have noticed in my life. Discipline is like those bridges that help me get to where I need to go. In order to repair the damage I need to build a bridge of discipline to get me there. In fact, any time I need to get somewhere difficult, discipline is usually the bridge I must cross to get there. Here's what I know about the discipline bridge. It takes time and effort to build it, but once this bridge is in place it actually makes the journey easy. I can get back and forth with ease.

Think about the time you first learned to drive a car. In the beginning, you had to think about everything you did. You were conscious of steering, shifting gears, signaling, braking and accelerating. It might have even felt overwhelming if you had to learn to drive a stick shift. So many things to remember! However, over time, discipline took over. All those behaviors moved from your conscious mind to your subconscious mind. After a while, people don't even think about what they do when they drive a car. Practice and discipline were the bridges that made the journey easy. It's the same way with sports. Accomplished athletes have built habits into their lives over the years. It is second nature. Serena Williams finds it harder to make a poor shot in tennis than a good one because she's trained herself so well, for so long. She has practiced that forehand so much that it's part of her subconscious. She has to consciously try to make a bad shot.

We will not look like Serena Williams our second time out on the tennis court. Discipline is the bridge that will get us there, and it takes a little while to build. At first, being disciplined seems hard—like you are adding one more item on your daily list of chores. But that's not true. Over time, discipline is a bridge, not a burden. It makes the journey easier if you'll hang with it. It becomes a part of you.

Growing up, my hero was Pete Rose. I followed every game he played, and believed he would one day be the all-time hit king. In his autobiography called *My Prison Without Bars,* Rose confessed to gambling—betting on games his own team played.[vii] It is the unpardonable sin in baseball. In the book he admitted he was aware of his privileges, but not his responsibilities. That's the issue—feeling we are above the rules in certain categories of our life. Rose writes, "I was aware of my records and my place in baseball history. But I was never aware of boundaries or able to control that part of my life. Admitting that I was out of control has been next to impossible for me."[viii] He asks, "How could I be so disciplined on one part of my life—and so reckless in another?"[ix]

The key is to develop a disciplined life. To simply have disciplined compartments in your life won't help you in the end. It needs to be a lifestyle. Today, we are interested in our image more than our integrity. Remember—the word "integrity" means to be whole, not divided. It is the opposite of hypocrisy. Image is about how we look or appear. It is superficial. There are millions of Americans whose discipline is only about image. Therefore, it only affects one part of their life. A few years ago, we all began hearing about the exercise program P90X®. While it's a great program, the "ab" workout is for aesthetics, not athletics. Excuse me, but being ripped is all for show. It does not mean we are better athletes.

In 2003, several athletes were paid big money for celebrity endorsements before they ever accomplished anything professionally. *USA Today* asked the question: "Does Madison Avenue care about real achievement anymore? 'Winning just doesn't matter as much as it used to,' says Jim Andrews, editorial director of the IEG

Sponsorship Report. 'There are other ways these athletes can capture the public's attention: by being gorgeous or by being a bad boy.' And getting the public's attention is all these companies really care about."[x]

How sad that image is more important than integrity to so many. Discipline for the purpose of image is a false bridge. It won't get you where you want to go. If you use this false bridge to get you from your desires to your goals, you'll find that it will someday collapse. Why? It's not real. Real discipline *impacts function*, not just form, and should affect your *whole life*. It will get you from desire to reality. You won't just look better—you'll live better. It is a long bridge. It won't get you there overnight. Psychologists suggest it takes at least fourteen days of discipline to build a good habit. But stay on it, and you'll find yourself getting past the damage of personal tornadoes. You'll be able to repair what's been harmed along the way.

A Look at the Book

There's an old proverb that says, "He who hates discipline, despises himself." An undisciplined person eventually has no self-respect. Without discipline, you'll eventually stop liking who you are.

Discipline is part of every effective leader's life, even for Christians. The opposite of grace is works, but not effort. II Peter 1:5 tells us to "make every effort to support your faith with diligence." The word "diligence" is often translated "virtue" and literally means excellence, something that functions well on the inside. Discipline means changing from the inside out. What does this mean to you?

Check out 1 Corinthians 9:24-27:

> *Do you not know that those who run in a race all run, but only one receives the prize? Run in such a way that you may win. And everyone who competes in the games exercises self-control in all things. They then do it to receive a perishable wreath, but we an imperishable. Therefore, I run in such a way as not without aim; I box in such a way as not beating the air; but I buffet my body and make it my slave, lest possibly after I have preached to others, I myself should be disqualified.*

What does Paul compare our discipline to?

In which areas of your life do you lack discipline?

_____

_____

_____

Getting Personal

As you consider your life today, you probably see some areas of your life that are disciplined and some that are not. We usually find it easier to be disciplined in the areas of our passion or interest. However, true discipline becomes a lifestyle that helps you in every area: what you eat, how you connect with people, your exercise and health, your thought patterns and more. Choose two or three important areas of your life and evaluate your level of discipline based on key areas:

1. Delayed gratification
I can delay pleasures I want; I experience self-control; I can wait for rewards until the timing is right.

1   2   3   4   5   6   7   8   9   10
<IMMEDIATE GRATIFICATION   DELAYED GRATIFICATION>

2. Holistic approach
I'm not just disciplined in one area of my life, discipline _is_ my lifestyle; it's a rule, not an exception.

1   2   3   4   5   6   7   8   9   10
<COMPARTMENTALIZED   HOLISTIC>

3. Functional training
I experience discipline for a legitimate function; it's about integrity, not image or appearance.

1   2   3   4   5   6   7   8   9   10
<I'M MOTIVATED BY IMAGE   I'M MOTIVATED BY INTEGRITY>

Practicing the Truth

Think about an area of your life that you consider undisciplined. Write it down. Next, write down one tangible step you could take to build discipline in that area. Next, find someone to hold you accountable to do that one step for fourteen days. Invite them to ask you about it daily. Finally, evaluate if this step helps you to discipline other areas of your life as well. Think of other areas you could build discipline. Begin a habit of discipline—you can usually create new habits in two weeks' time. Discipline will be the bridge to get you where you want to go.

The Half-Hearted Kamikaze

KAMIKAZE PILOTS ARE ONLY USEFUL IF THEY ARE COMMITTED TO THEIR MISSION. LEADERS ARE THE SAME WAY. YOU CANNOT HAVE INVOLVEMENT WITHOUT COMMITMENT AND BE EFFECTIVE. IT GOES WITH THE TERRITORY.

I love this story of a kamikaze pilot who flew in World War II for the Japanese Air Force. He was interviewed by a newspaper reporter after returning from his fiftieth mission. The reporter asked the pilot if he wasn't a contradiction in terms. How can someone be a kamikaze pilot—whose mission is to fly into military bases and give up their life in the process—and still be alive after fifty missions?

"Well it's like this," the pilot responded. "I was very involved. Not very committed, but very involved."

I always smile when I think of this story. A true kamikaze pilot only flies on one mission. He gives his life for that one mission. He cannot be involved without being committed. There's no such thing as a half-hearted kamikaze. Commitment goes with the territory. And so it is with us. If we have any hope of being a successful person, much less an effective leader, we must be committed. Leaders possess commitment. They cannot be involved without being committed. The rest of the world may enjoy involvement without commitment, but we cannot, as emerging leaders.

What's the difference between involvement and commitment? Just think about a pig and a chicken, after eating a ham and egg breakfast. The chicken was involved. The pig was committed!

The word "mediocre" was first used to describe rock (or mountain) climbers who were involved but not committed. The word literally means "middle of the rock." It was used to describe climbers who started a climb to the top but didn't finish. They stopped halfway. Ouch. Sound familiar?

Our communities, school campuses and offices are filled with folks who are involved but not really committed. They want to keep all their options open, and often don't make decisions until the last minute because a better opportunity may arise at the eleventh hour. In fact, because our world offers us so many options, we tend to not commit ourselves because we don't want to narrow our focus. We want to do it all! The problem is, we can't do it all. I have said many times: leaders can do anything, but they can't do everything. Nearly every great leader in history accomplished something memorable because of a narrow focus, and a great commitment to a cause. Even young leaders have figured this out and made their mark because they got committed.

Joan of Arc knew her life mission by the time she was fifteen years old. At seventeen, she led 3,000 French knights in battle. On one occasion, she told a military general, "I will lead the way over the wall." The general replied, "Not a man will follow you." Joan of Arc said, "I won't be looking back to see if they're following me."

At nineteen she was burned alive because she would not recant on her commitment to France. The British gave her a chance to regain her liberty if she would only change her allegiance, but she would not. In choosing to die at the stake she said, "Everyone gives their life for what they believe. Sometimes people believe in little or nothing and yet they give their life to that little or nothing. One life is all we have, and we live it, and then it's gone. But to give up what you are and to live without belief is more terrible than dying, even more terrible than dying young."

John Wesley founded the organization that later became the Methodist Church when he was seventeen. He could have done many other things. He was educated at Oxford and enjoyed horticulture, medicine, journalism, and politics. But he saw the great spiritual need of England during the 18th century and committed himself to spiritual renewal. He traveled over 250,000 miles on horseback, teaching and organizing churches for more than fifty years. Unlike Joan of Arc, Wesley died of old age, but not until his movement had impacted Great Britain. One history book reported that John Wesley almost single-handedly saved England from bloody revolution.

How Commitment Works

Today, people talk about commitments they're going to make, but often fail to keep them. New Years resolutions last until February or March at best. We say we believe in something or we make a promise—then we drift from it. Talk is cheap. Half-hearted kamikazes are a dime a dozen. The reason other folks live such quality lives and possess such great influence is that they do more than talk. They're committed to some ideals, and they live them out. They move from a "wish" to a "lifestyle" by surrendering to a cause along the way. There are phases we usually experience as we build commitment in our lives. It starts with an idea and ends with a conviction:

1. Ideas: *We perceive an issue by the way we think about it. This involves our minds.*

2. Opinions: *We begin to express our preferences on that issue. This involves our emotions.*

3. Beliefs: *We conclude where we stand on the issue. This involves both mind and emotions.*

4. Commitments: *We begin to act on our belief. This involves our mind, emotions and will.*

5. Convictions: *We are ready to die for our commitment. It now is a passion in our lives.*

Your commitment will mean something when you act on it for an extended period of time. When you become committed, you will notice something wonderful. The moment you make a commitment you will find all kinds of wisdom, energy, and resources at your disposal that weren't necessarily there before you committed yourself. Commitment opens up the floodgates to the resources you need—but they won't show up a moment too soon. Many people want to see everything in place before they get committed. Unfortunately, they will never act if they are waiting for perfect conditions. They are half-hearted kamikazes. Others wait for a feeling before they act. They want to "feel" led to do something. Once again, they may be waiting for a while. We are much more likely to act our way into a feeling, than we are to feel our way into action. Get committed long enough, and eventually that commitment will become a conviction you'll be willing to die for.

A Look at the Book

Check out Matthew 16:24:

> *If any one wants to come after Me, let him deny himself, take up his cross and follow Me.*

Several times Jesus clarified what it meant to be His disciple. He wanted us to make no mistake about it: belonging to him would cost us.

Jesus gives us three simple statements that sum up commitment:

• Sacrifice: Deny yourself… (Set aside your own pleasures and comfort.)

• Purpose: Take up your cross… (Find your reason for God placing you on earth.)

• Determination: Follow me. (Follow through on your decisions until they are complete.)

Which is most difficult for you to live out as a young leader: sacrifice, purpose or determination?

_____

_____

Why do you think Jesus kept clarifying the commitment His followers would need to make?

_____

_____

_____

Why is it difficult for you to make long-term commitments?

_____

_____

_____

Getting Personal

Review the five phases of building personal convictions: ideas, opinions, beliefs, commitments, convictions. Now reflect on two decisions you've made recently. The decisions should involve some future plan. Was it difficult to follow through on them? Where do you stand on those two decisions? List these two decisions and circle the stage you think you are in on each of them:

DECISION:

_____

STAGE: IDEA   OPINION   BELIEF   COMMITMENT   CONVICTION

DECISION:

_____

STAGE: IDEA   OPINION   BELIEF   COMMITMENT   CONVICTION

Practicing the Truth

Make a list of some past promises you've made to yourself or others. Be sure to include some you failed to keep. Next, select one of those unkept promises and determine to keep that promise for two whole weeks. Fix your eyes on a clear goal. Write it down and write out the benefit of reaching that goal. Ask someone to hold you accountable to reach it. Discuss the process. How does this affect your character? How does it deepen your integrity? If you're part of a team, initiate the same process with your teammates. What makes fulfilling a commitment so difficult? What will it take to follow through on a tough one?

Drivers and Passengers

WHEN LIFE GOES BAD, PEOPLE BLAME SOMEONE ELSE FOR THE PROBLEM. THEY ACT
LIKE PASSENGERS. LEADERS REALIZE THEY ARE DRIVERS—AND ARE RESPONSIBLE
FOR THEIR ATTITUDES AND DESTINATION IN LIFE.

Soon after my daughter Bethany turned fifteen, she began the pursuit of a driver's
permit. Or, should I say, "we" began the pursuit. It was a family affair. It was amazing
how I struggled through the pains of letting go, and turning over the wheel and
the keys to my "baby." I knew it was time to let go, it was just hard. My job was to
pass on responsibility, and her job was to take it on.

Bethany ended up developing her driving skills in both my car and my wife's
minivan. Early in the process we delivered to her the infamous lecture on "drivers
and passengers." (You may have given it—many parents share this little talk at some
point in the process.) It is a little "sermon" on the differences between being a driver
and being a passenger. It goes something like this:

"So far, all your life has been spent as a passenger. You've been able to let your mind
wander, to change CDs in the player, locate new radio stations, sing, shout, laugh
and get distracted to your heart's content. Why? Because you're just along for the
ride. Your goal was to make the ride fun.

"Things are different now. It's not that the ride won't be fun—it's just that 'fun' isn't
the goal anymore. You are a driver now. The steering wheel is in your hands, and
so are the rest of the passengers in that car. Both the machine we call an automobile
and all the humans on board are at your mercy. Because of that you must act like
the owner of the car, not a guest. You must play the part of manager of the store,
not just an employee. You are a driver now. It may mean you can't do whatever you
want at any moment, like adjust your iPod playlist, wave to friends or let your mind
wander. You must think about where you are going and about the well-being of the
passengers in the car with you. You are the one responsible for getting to the
destination. You are a driver now."

Being a driver is about responsibility. It's about ownership. It is a life lesson some people never learn. When life goes wrong, many people blame others for the problem.

"If my wife would only..."

"If my husband would just stop..."

"If my supervisor only started..."

"If my children didn't..."

"If my department weren't so..."

Individuals who do not take responsibility for actions become victims who have no control over their attitudes or their destination. They are passengers in life. Leaders do not fall prey to this victim mindset. It isn't that they are in denial. Leaders understand some things do go wrong. However, they determine to remain drivers. They take responsibility for their attitude and their responses to problems. They take responsibility for the direction of their life. Let me suggest three areas leaders choose to be drivers and refuse to be passengers:

• Positive attitude (Their thinking and perspective on life)
• Persistent fortitude (Their determination in response to tough situations)
• Purposeful latitude (Their flexibility based on a clear focus on future direction)

Dawn Loggins grew up in a ramshackle home in North Carolina, with no electricity or running water. Her parents were drug addicts and took little responsibility for their kids. During Dawn's senior year in high school, she came home from school one day to find her parents had abandoned her. Suddenly, Dawn was homeless.

She made a decision very rapidly. She didn't want the lifestyle her parents had modeled for her—a volatile life of ups and downs, living hand to mouth. So she began sleeping at friends' homes, and got a job as a janitor at her high school. She showed up early to mop floors, clean restrooms, and wipe down chalkboards…all the while reviewing for tests she herself would take in those classrooms.

Let's face it. This is a scenario where it would have been easy for Dawn to draw a welfare check and simply give up. Driven by a life she did not want, however, Dawn just plain took responsibility for her life. She feels sorry for her parents, but the whole episode has served to ignite her ambition to make something of herself. She not only works before and after school, but studies hard and makes straight A's. Just recently, Dawn applied and was accepted to Harvard University. Amazing. This girl will go from "homeless to Harvard."

Why Leaders Must Model This

Few things disturb followers more than a leader who fails to take responsibility for his actions. Intuitively, people expect leaders to be "drivers," not passengers. This explains the feeling most Americans had during the Monica Lewinsky scandal in 1998. President Clinton had told everyone that he had not had sex with the White House intern. In August of 1998, he was forced to admit he had engaged in sexual activity with her. This was enough to trouble some. However, the alarming point came when he gave his five-minute speech, confessing the whole thing. The majority of people I spoke with (both Republicans and Democrats) were disappointed in the speech. A reporter examined the speech and uncovered why we felt the way we did:

Total number of words he used in the speech: 549 words.

Number of words devoted to self-justification: 134 words.

Number of words devoted to regret for actions: 4 words.

Number of words devoted to attack on the prosecutor: 180 words.

Number of words devoted to saying it's time to move on: 137 words.

Number of words devoted to apology: none.

After the speech, most Americans agreed that something was conspicuously absent. We all know good leadership when we see it and when we don't. President Clinton had wonderful charisma as a leader, but failed on that evening to demonstrate character. Things might have been different had he said, "I take full responsibility for my actions. I blame no one. I acted immorally and I lied to my country. I have wronged my wife. I have wronged my daughter. I have wronged America. As your leader, I apologize and seek your forgiveness." What America needed in that moment wasn't charisma. We needed character.

History teaches us that America is very forgiving to a leader who owns up to his or her actions. Just ask John F. Kennedy. After his biggest presidential mistake, the Bay of Pigs fiasco, he assumed full responsibility for it. His popularity actually went up. In fact, he said later: "I don't understand it. The more mistakes I make, the more they like me." In reality, it wasn't the mistakes we liked, it was the exhibition of integrity. People felt they could trust him. He was a driver, not a passenger. That is my challenge for you, the rest of your life.

A Look at the Book

Check out Matthew 21:28-31. It says:

> But what do you think? A man had two sons, and he came to the first and said, "Son, go work today in the vineyard." And he answered and said, "I will sir;" and he did not go. And the man came to his second and said the same thing. But he answered and said, "I will not;" yet he afterward regretted it and went. Which of the two did the will of his father? They said, "The latter." Jesus said to them, "Truly I say to you, that the tax gatherers and harlots will get into the Kingdom of God before you."

What is the difference between the two sons? Both of them say one thing and do another. What makes them different?

_____

_____

_____

What is Jesus getting at in this passage? What is He trying to communicate that is important?

_____

_____

_____

Do you identify with the first son at all? In what situations do you say you'll do something and then fail to do it? Why do you think you fail? How is that like being a passenger instead of a driver?

_____

_____

_____

Getting Personal

The Great Wall of China is one of the Seven Wonders of the World. Do you know its history? It was originally built centuries ago to keep out all invading armies. It was built so tall and so wide, no army could penetrate it. At least, that's what they thought. The Chinese were successfully invaded three times during the first one hundred years. In none of those cases, however, did the enemy climb the wall, or tunnel through it. In every case…they simply bribed the guards at the gate.

What an illustration for us today. We spend so much time, effort and money attempting to create programs to solve our problems. We work on the "outside" to prevent anything bad from happening. Unfortunately, we fail to address the real need inside our hearts.

In what areas of your life have you failed to be a driver? Where have you become a victim, or a "passenger," and allowed circumstances to determine where your life has gone? List them below.

_____

_____

_____

_____

_____

In each of these areas you listed, what's one decision that would help enable you to be a driver? List those decisions below.

_____

_____

_____

_____

_____

PRACTICING THE TRUTH

Sometimes the scariest thing for people to do is to raise money from people they don't know. It is a test of courage and initiative. Choose a charity you really believe in. If you don't know of any, check some out on the Internet. Then, go raise $1,000 for this worthwhile organization. Make a list of people you can talk to, and what you'll say when you discuss the project. Then, take time this week to approach these people with your idea and request. Choose to be a driver and see this little project through.

DROPPING OUR EXCUSES FOR NOT BEING A DRIVER

In 2013, the world heard about a twenty-year-old student in Hong Kong named Tsang Tsz-Kwan. She's severely hearing-impaired and blind, and she has limited sensitivity in her fingers—but she taught herself to read Braille…with her lips. Yep, you read that right. Not only that—she's become an amazing success, scoring within the top 5% in almost all of the subjects on her college entrance exam. With her disabilities, she could have opted to not take the tests—but to her, that was not an option.

"I have to accept I'm disadvantaged … I decided to take the challenge whatever the results," she said. "I think the most important thing is the courage to face the challenge."[xi]

That's the kind of statement you make when you're a driver, not just some passenger, in life.

[End Notes]

i   Jacobs, Emma. "A father who saw untapped forces in his son's autism." *Financial Times,* June 6, 2013. http://www.ft.com/intl/cms/s/0/ba2d5706-ccf5-11e2-9efe-00144feab7de.html

ii Joshua Kurlantzick, "Liar, Liar." *Entrepreneur,* October 1, 2003. http://www.entrepreneur.com/article/printthis/64464.html

iii Nell Minow, *The Movie Mom's Guide to Family Movies,* (New York: Avon Books, 1999), 63.

iv Indiana University, "Violent Video Games May Emotionally Arouse Players," January 23, 2007. http://newsinfo.iu.edu/web/page/print/4685.html

v   Van Valkenburg, Kevin. "Have faith in Barrett Jones." *ESPN The Magazine* 22 Apr. 2013. Web. http://espn.go.com/nfl/draft2013/story/_/id/9197435/2013-nfl-draft-alabama-barrett-jones-espn-magazine

vi Gardner, David. "Honest Japanese return $78million in cash found in earthquake rubble." *Mail Online,* August 17, 2011. http://www.dailymail.co.uk/news/article-2027129/Honest-Japanese-return-78million-cash-earthquake-rubble.html

vii Pete Rose and Rick Hill, *My Prison Without Bars,* (Emmaus, PA: Rodale, 2004).

viii Pete Rose, "Exclusive: Pete Rose's Confession." *Sports Illustrated,* January 12, 2004. http://sportsillustrated.cnn.com/vault/article/magazine/MAG1031062/1/index.htm

ix Ronald Blum, "Belligerent Rose only a bit apologetic." *Amarillo Globe-News,* January 9, 2004. http://amarillo.com/stories/010904/spo_rosebook.shtml

x   Michael McCarthy, "Win or lose, drawing endorsements is key; Celebrity is big part of game." *USA Today,* August 22, 2003, B1.

xi "Tsang Tsz-Kwan, Blind Student With Limited Finger Sensitivity, Reads Braille With Her Lips, And Kicks Academic Butt (VIDEO)." *Huffington Post,* July 18, 2013. http://www.huffingtonpost.com/2013/07/18/tsan-tsz-kwan-blind-student-reads-braille-with-lips_n_3619430.html